RACINE: LANGUAGE AND THEATRE

FM12

RACINE

LANGUAGE AND THEATRE

BY
HENRY PHILLIPS

UNIVERSITY OF DURHAM 1994

ISBN 0 907310 29 X

Acknowledgements

I should like to thank Peter Bayley, Denys Potts and especially Jonathan Mallinson for reading my book in its various draft stages and for their helpful advice and encouragement. I am also grateful to the University of Cambridge and Emmanuel College for a prolonged period of sabbatical leave during which this book was completed.

CONTENTS

Introduction

The focus of this study is essentially the act of speaking and the degree to which the characters' concerns which derive from speaking (and indeed listening) contribute to the promotion of tragic effect. It is remarkable in fact to what extent characters talk about talking. The need to speak, clearly enhanced by the nature of what is to be said, is a constant source of anxiety. The possibility or the inescapability of entering into dialogue with others, or the thought that dialogue may come to an end, are in themselves productive of extreme emotion. Moreover, the characters know that the very act of speaking is fraught with danger because what they say has or could have grave consequences for themselves and others. At the same time, their manner of speech may be as revealing as the content of their speeches. In that sense, Racinian tragedy may be considered dramatic less for its account of human motivations, character or passion than for the tragic implications with which Racine invests the speech act. If one holds to this particular perspective, speech is at the root of the tragic experience rather than the vehicle for providing an account of it. Racine's plays explore therefore what I would like to call the tension of utterance.

Previous studies of Racinian language have had different priorities. They have been concerned with verbal forms (Ratermanis), poetry (Vinaver), rhetoric (France and Hawcroft), or stylistic effects of various sorts (Spitzer).[1] My own priority has been rather to concentrate exclusively on aspects of speech and on the ways in which the characters are conscious of the consequences of articulating their emotions to others. I am not therefore concerned with an analysis of those emotions themselves or the more general context of the characters' situation, for example in relation to fate. This is of course not to claim any exclusivity of approach or to deny the legitimacy of other points of view. It is simply that, looked at from the point of view of the tension of utterance, Racinian drama can be interpreted as enacting states of speech rather than states of mind and as conveying a tragedy of communication.

A further possibility in offering this approach to Racinian tragedy is that it roots the plays directly in a *theatrical* perspective. In other words the anxieties at the root of speech and the tension of utterance I have mentioned focus on performance. Certainly Michael Hawcroft's excellent analysis of the way the characters argue and the way they respond to argument offers one view of theatricality. But the traditional framework of rhetoric does not take account of a deeper form of theatricality, where anxiety about the act of speaking is apparent at the inception of speech. My approach has regard to what might be called the existential nature of the speech act.

Such a view of Racinian tragedy may indeed help in providing a definition of what constitutes action in the plays. Although the signs are that the situation is improving, English-speaking audiences especially have been notoriously reluctant to recognise that things happen in Racinian drama. Too often action is regarded as physical action and its absence is bemoaned. David Maskell has to a certain extent put paid to that complaint by detailing most impressively levels of physical action that are incorporated in one way or another in the texts. In my own perspective, speaking constitutes a series of events which can be clearly delineated in the course of the action. Very often, it might be possible to argue, tragedy occurs less for what has been said than because it has been said at all. An important barrier has been crossed, the barrier between silence and speech. Speech is therefore an irreducibly physical act. A voice has been heard, feelings have been voiced, which should not have been. Speech is physical action.

This very point will allow me eventually to broaden the implications of Racinian tragedy. In his concentration on aspects of performance, which derives from the characters' awareness of how things have been or must be said, Racine elaborates a problematics of speaking and listening which, I will argue, become a reflexion on the act of theatre itself. Performance, as Racinian characters know, involves risk. Actors know that too, once they themselves have broken the barrier between silence and language. The problems of Racine's characters are therefore actor's problems. Looked at in this way, Racine points us to a notion of theatricality which endows his tragedies with a significance beyond an examination of the human condition. That is achieved through the importance Racine places on acts of speech.

What I have called the existential aspect of acts of speech in Racine is the subject of Chapter 2 where I analyse the way the characters prepare themselves for speaking and the ways in which they reveal their anxieties about it. I shall also deal with the way the characters prepare themselves for listening, since one of the key aspects of Racinian drama is the degree to which the characters expect and desire to hear certain things. Hence Racine emphasises the importance of presence, that is to say where meetings between the characters are seen in terms of an imperative. However, no account of speech in Racine's plays could be complete without a consideration of silence. But silence will be seen to consist not only in the absence of speech but in the absence of the right sort of speech.

Chapter 3 will explore specific ways in which characters attempt to avoid speech through using a substitute, in other words where characters speak for others, as messengers for example. Here the concept of 'speaking as one', that is to say where the messenger and the message-giver say the same thing, will be seen to be important and will also provide a focus for situations where characters seek to differentiate their voice from that of others. But usurpation of voice will also constitute a major theme in those situations where some characters speak in the place of others. But various forms of substitution operate within the voice of a single character as well as between characters. Characters use different voices (for example, the voice of the lover, the voice of the emperor) according to different circumstances, to the extent that questions can be raised concerning what actually constitutes 'character', particularly in terms of continuity or discontinuity.

Another important aspect of acts of speech in Racinian tragedy, discussed in Chapter 4, is that they have a particular relevance to time not only in the present but to time in the past and the future. To what extent does past speech constitute a commitment, for example through promises and oaths? Can characters who have engaged in dialogue in the past take up where they have left off? Does dialogue have continuity therefore? On the other hand, dialogue between characters can be created in the course of the action where it has not existed previously. For all the characters the future of dialogue is important. This is especially so if, as I claim, speech is life for the characters. Their existence outside speech constitutes an undifferentiated time. Time is therefore speech time. But I should also like to introduce a concept where the characters can be considered 'out of time', where even in speech there is no life.

All these aspects of speech in the tragedies need to be situated in the overall framework within which Racine organises and patterns the dialogue in the plays, and that is the subject of Chapter 1. The question of the imperative of presence I have mentioned earlier and the notion of expectation, an essential element of the conditions of speech in Racine, are underpinned by the ways in which the relationships between the characters are determined by their place in what I have called sets and axes of communication. I shall also consider questions arising from the characters' status within the conditions of speech at key moments of the action, something which is clearly related to the tension of utterance and anxiety that is at the root of Racinian speech. Finally, some discussion of divergent, convergent and shared discourse will help in appreciating the issues raised in the beginning of Chapter 3.

It may be argued that what I have to say could be said of any playwright, either in the seventeenth century or since. I would reply that no other playwright, certainly of the period, foregrounds the problems I outline in quite the same explicit way. Racine heightens our awareness of the interface with the world which is constituted by language. How we speak to one another in certain types of situation comes under the closest scrutiny. Talking about ourselves to others. A simple but powerful theme.[2]

Chapter 1
The Conditions of Speech

As I have made clear in the introduction to this study of Racine's tragedies, my emphasis will be on acts of speech and the ways in which, in themselves, they contribute to what is tragic about the situations of the characters. In this chapter I should like to look at how Racine builds into the *structure* of his plays the importance of acts of speech as determinant factors in the tragedies. That is to say that the tension of utterance to which I have referred is directly underpinned by the structuring of the meetings and the groupings of the characters upon which the patterning of the dialogue is based. Many of the themes of later chapters such as expectation, presence, situations where characters speak for others and pressure of time in the context of speech will refer back to this patterning of dialogue. In other words the tension of utterance derives from the effectiveness with which Racine brings the characters together and the conditions in which they appear together, what I have called the conditions of speech. These conditions of speech thus determine in some way how characters reflect themselves on what they have to say and whether they are prepared to say it.

The essential nature of the conditions of speech in Racinian tragedy is first and foremost that of a transaction where the characters have to negotiate with one another. The organisation of dialogue is thus built round that transaction and is directed towards a conclusion. At this level the drama ensues from a situation where different sets of characters envisage different conclusions and, in general terms, tragedy arises from the conflict of those conclusions. Characters attempt to persuade one another that one conclusion must prevail over all others. It is often the case for example that marriage will be insisted upon by one character with another, and that arguments will be deployed against that conclusion. In this sense, an important element of the Racinian transaction is its specificity. Characters know exactly what is at stake in each scene where they engage in dialogue because they have to address the conclusion envisaged by other characters or they have to persuade of the legitimacy of their own conclusion. Thus Racine sets up patterns of expectation by the very fact that, when two characters meet, they generally, although not in all cases, know something about what they will hear.

One could say then that Racine's plays, centred as they are on a single issue, or on issues related to a central point (there are no sub-plots as such in Racinian drama), contain a project of some sort according to which the dialogue is patterned. We could take *Iphigénie* as an example of a Racinian project in its purest form. In order to produce the wind necessary to speed the Greeks on their way to Troy, a sacrifice must be carried out, and the person to be sacrificed is the daughter of Agamemnon. The whole of the negotiation among the characters centres on cooperation with or opposition to that project. Characters are thus neatly divided into two camps, those who wish the project to succeed and those who do not. Each scene is without equivocation or ambiguity directed towards that single issue. *Britannicus* too adopts this structure in that the two camps are represented by the mother, Agrippine, and the son, Néron respectively. The issue is their continued separation or reconciliation. All negotiations in the play are organised around the conflict involved in the realisation of the conclusions envisaged by those two characters.

Other plays are not so straightforward in the way the project or central issue can be outlined, and the pattern of negotiation is a complex one. *Andromaque* is a particularly good example of this complexity. In one sense the central transaction of the play is the deepening gulf between the Greeks and Pyrrhus. But this does not adequately take account of Andromaque herself. In fact four different characters have four different projects which have to be negotiated, each of them getting in the way of the others. Pyrrhus wants to marry his captive: Hermione wants to marry Pyrrhus; Oreste wants to take Hermione with him from Epirus; and Andromaque wishes to save her son without a marriage which is contrary to her fidelity to Hector.

With *Mithridate* and *Phèdre* a certain complexity in the situation of negotiation emerges from the sudden change in circumstances effected by the respective returns of Mithridate and Thésée. No individual project seems to concern Mithridate for the first three scenes, although his presence even through absence is keenly felt. Monime's intention at this stage is self-protection while that of Xipharès is to declare his love for her. Pharnace, who in himself soon becomes incidental to the action, wishes to take the place of his father as Monime's betrothed. The action then involves the characters we see at the beginning of the play in negotiating terms of survival. Mithridate's project becomes the attempt to discover precisely what has happened. The situation is complicated by Monime's albeit reluctant insistence to Xipharès that she must comply with Mithridate's original intention to marry her. Another layer of complication is added, however, by the fact that Xipharès shares the same political aspirations as his father, while being a rival in love. His difficulties are compounded by Mithridate making him the guardian of Monime whom he suspects of complicity with Pharnace. This configuration of events and beliefs forces Monime to confess her love for Xipharès to the prince himself, a confession full of danger for her.

What in *Phédre* can be described as the central project around which all negotiations centre? In the first two Acts two sets of characters seem to move in separate worlds, on the one hand Hippolyte and Aricie, on the other Phèdre. Like Mithridate, Thésée's project is to discover why all the characters seem reluctant to stay with him at his return. In fact it could be argued that the speech of the other characters all relates to him from that point since, of course, Hippolyte and Phèdre are together only once more in the same space (Act III, scene 4), and then simply to be present at Thésée's entrance (they do not speak to each other). The project of each of the characters is to convince the king. With both *Mithridate* and *Phèdre* we are some way from the project as it can be formulated in its purest form exemplified in *Iphigénie.*

As I have remarked earlier, the project of the plays, whatever its degree of complexity or simplicity, is such that the objective at each stage of the negotiations between the characters is usually clear for the spectator as far as one at least of the characters is concerned. It is the usual pattern in Racinian tragedy that confrontations between major characters do not impart information we are not aware of in some way prior to their happening. There are no surprises for the spectator. This is sometimes true of the characters. With Pyrrhus the objective is always the persuasion of Hector's widow to accept the king's proposal of marriage. The terms of the debate are based on a premiss which has been clearly stated prior to the two characters meeting. In some scenes in other plays the objective of one character, however clear to us, comes as a surprise to the other character involved in the dialogue. Some declarations of love fall into this category, as for example the most celebrated, Phèdre's declaration to Hippolyte. Equally surprising for Junie is Néron's declaration in *Britannicus.* The spectator is thus in a position to *see* how some characters listen to what they do not expect to hear. The conditions of speech thus constitute a sort of spectacle in themselves.

A corollary to the specific nature of the transaction is that, whatever the surprise of the other character involved, the reponse of that character cannot avoid addressing the issue that has been raised. In addition the receiver of the proposition at hand *must* act on what is said, either in acceptance or refusal, there being no time for compromise in clarifying a position one way or the other. This engages the immediate responsibility of the receiver. In effect Junie seals the fate of Britannicus in her refusal or even reluctance to comply with Néron's wishes (her love is manifest to Néron even in her apparent dismissal of Britannicus). Speech in Racine is therefore consequential at all stages of the negotiation, either for oneself or for others, or for everyone.[1] That pressure, in the course of which mistakes can be made, is the hallmark of Racinian tragedy, especially in view of the need for the negotiation to take place within a limited time span.

The pressure on the characters is further enhanced by the limited number of occasions on which characters meet each other. An analysis of the plays in this regard is quite instructive. As I have already mentioned, Phèdre and Hippolyte are on stage together for two scenes, during one of which they do not speak to each other. Agrippine and Néron meet twice on stage (Act IV, scene 2 and Act V, scene 6). Bérénice and Titus come together in Act II, scene 4, Act IV, scene 5 and then from Act V, scene 5 continuously for three scenes. Not only is time short in an absolute sense, but the opportunity for face to face persuasion is even shorter, especially if a mistake has been made, as Britannicus discovers in Act III, scene 7. The pressure of time is a point I shall explore more fully in Chapter 4.

This emphasis on time limits the degree to which characters can become acquainted in the course of the action. It is unusual in a Racinian tragedy (as indeed in most seventeenth-century tragedy) for complete strangers to meet. It is true that there is no evidence in *Andromaque* to suggest that Andromaque and Hermione have met before the third Act of the play, but they can hardly be said to be unknown to each other. The same is true of the relationships between Alexandre and the other characters, and of the relationship between Néron and Junie. To a certain extent therefore the situation of communication in the tragedies involves at the start a level of familiarity. It is to be imagined that there exists a degree to which the characters share the same context.

This is helped in the patterning of the dialogue by the existence of what might be called 'natural' sets of characters, that is to say characters for whom it is entirely natural to come together at some stage. The degree to which sets are stable or dissolve very much determines the success or failure of the transaction which forms the project I have referred to in the previous section. Sets may be based on nature itself. Fathers and sons, as with Hippolyte and Thésée, Mithridate and Xipharès and Pharnace: mothers and sons, as in *La Thébaïde* and *Britannicus*, and so on. Sets may also be constituted through requited love: Junie and Britannicus, for example, or through religious solidarity as with Joad and Abner. Some sets of characters are brought together by relations of power. Such is the case with Andromaque and Pyrrhus, and with Mithridate and Monime. Two other examples of this type of relationship are the sets Roxane / Bajazet and Néron / Junie. In these cases power on one side of the relationship creates necessity on the other. Bajazet depends for his life on pleasing Roxane. Eventually Andromaque is forced to act on the realisation that marriage to Pyrrhus is necessary if she is to save her son.

Not all sets represented in the plays are constituted before the action of the plays begins. Monime and Xipharès are unaware that their love is reciprocated. Aricie and Hippolyte 'find' each other. So sets can become 'naturalised' in the course of the tragedies where it is possible for dialogue to begin as well as to be a continuation of past speech. The relation of speech to the past, present and future is an important element of conditions of speech and will be developed in a later part of this study.

However 'natural' sets may appear to be, they are not without problems. Oreste and Hermione have constituted a set in the past which has been dissolved by the effects of the Trojan war. To what extent can they re-establish communication as lovers? How can they talk to each other as a couple? In another context, the same is true for Néron and Agrippine. Within the notion of natural sets, here established within nature itself, there is contained at least some notion of what we should expect from mother and son. In many forms of drama, and especially tragedy, the communication we find between them denies that expectation. The action of *Britannicus* becomes, as in *Andromaque*, the attempted reconstitution of communication within a natural set which has previously broken up. The most radical form of difficulty imaginable is dramatised in *La Thébaïde* where it could even be argued that the fundamental impossibilty of the re-establishment of communication between the two brothers (and hence all the other characters in the play — their ability to communicate is irrelevant without the reconciliation of Etéocle and Polynice) makes it an unpromising subject for drama. In Act IV, scene 3 the whole family is present on stage without the remotest chance of them speaking with one voice.

Family relationships make the set composed of Hippolyte and Phèdre particularly interesting. The set of which they are a part by virtue of Phèdre's declaration of love and its consequences is neither natural at the outset (she is his stepmother) nor in terms of love (it is incestuous). In fact Racine's last profane play seems to chart the progress of solution and dissolution in speech and dialogue from almost every angle. Aricie and Hippolyte should not in fact form a natural set because all men are forbidden to fall in love with Aricie. The set they do constitute can never be consummated through marriage because of the young prince's death. The natural set that should exist between Thésée and his son is dissolved through the father's renunciation and curse.

Indeed some sets perceived by others as natural turn out to be rather less so. Pyrrhus in fact regards Oreste and Hermione as a natural set:

> Ah! qu'ils s'aiment, Phoenix! J'y consens. Qu'elle parte.
> Que charmés l'un de l'autre ils retournent à Sparte. (ll. 253–54)

Hermione's *confidente,* Cléone, urges upon her that Oreste should become her natural interlocutor rather than Pyrrhus: 'Eh bien, Madame, eh bien! écoutez donc Oreste'. (l. 409) It should be borne in mind, of course, that Pyrrhus belongs to no 'natural' set since Hermione belongs to him as a tribute of war rather than as part of a natural relationship. In fact none of the characters in the play forms a natural set with another character in the proper sense of that term. In *Bérénice* Titus believes that he, Bérénice and Antiochus form a natural set and is later surprised to find that this is not the case.

Although the characters at one level are organised into sets according to various criteria, they do not remain discrete dramatic units. That is to say that, normally, they cannot on their own resolve an issue. A certain mobility of individuals within sets may be discerned whereby other characters are brought into an *axis of communication* whose members may share or have shared a common purpose or set of principles. A set may or may not in this sense constitute an axis of communication. Indeed *Britannicus* is a good example of a set (Agrippine and Néron) which no longer constitutes an axis of communication. It can turn out that sets which are not natural in terms of family or love come to form axes of communication in some way. Interestingly, Pyrrhus and Andromaque (and potentially Pyrrhus and Hermione) are axes of communication which can formulate a resolution, since a decision of either pair forecloses all other options. In Andromaque's case, the axis which includes the king is required if she is to negotiate successfully the survival of her son.

It cannot be said that Roxane and Atalide form a natural set and in any case they meet as a function of the relationship between Roxane and Bajazet rather than because they both share an interest in each other. However, with Bajazet, they form the indispensable axis of communication necessary to the understanding of the development of the relationship between Roxane and

Bajazet (the action of the play in fact represents the end of the axis they previously formed together — Roxane now wants to see Bajazet alone). The irony is that Roxane has encouraged an independent axis to form around the set of Bajazet / Atalide, although, again, it must be emphasised that this set on its own cannot bring about a solution. Indeed the example of Roxane and Atalide serves to show to what extent relationships in Racine are based first and foremost on the network of negotiation that exists in the plays.

In introducing the notion of axes of communication I mentioned the mobility of characters between different axes, indeed even between different sets. Hermione, for example, shifts between Oreste and Pyrrhus in the course of the action. Both sets, however, can in this case reach a conclusion. Neither Andromaque nor Oreste himself has any choice in which axis they finally settle on. Rival axes of communication exist for Iphigénie, since Clytemnestre, Achille and she form one, while Agamemnon, Ulysse and Calchas form the other. Eventually she adopts the latter axis even though one might consider that it is not most obviously in her interests. This is the only axis that can bring the action to a proper conclusion, especially since it involves Iphigénie's acquiescence. On the other hand Agamemnon's place in that axis is the result of necessity. He does not wish to bring about the sacrifice of his daughter.

I have made the point earlier that sets may come into being in the course of the action of a play. Of necessity this must also be true of axes of communication. Agrippine is forced to recognise that a new axis emerges with Néron's abduction of Junie, since a resolution to the action could be effected without the intervention of Agrippine (the people want Néron to rule in his own right). She, for political reasons, has always maintained another axis including Britannicus, Néron's potential rival as emperor. Previously Néron has been a part if not a prisoner of his mother's axis. As we shall see later, Néron wishes to adopt a language through which he can achieve independence and chooses to do this through his passion for Junie. His wife, Octavie (with whom Junie identifies), has always been a part of his mother's axis. What is important here is that the establishment of a new axis of communication entails the elimination of individuals from the old one, in this case Agrippine and eventually Britannicus. The irony is that Agrippine has herself chosen those who now advise Néron against linking his interests with hers (ll. 1149sq). Her conditions for restoring the axis of communication with Néron involve in their turn the exclusion of Junie and Burrhus (1280–85). It is again with some irony that in the very last scene, Burrhus and Agrippine form a new axis as a rival to that of Néron (ll. 1755–57).

Bajazet is another case where new axes of communication are created. Roxane has in effect cut herself loose from the axis she formed with Amurat in order to create one between herself and Bajazet. This includes all the other characters, since they depend for their survival on her success in promoting Bajazet as an alternative sultan. There is no real alternative, since the couple Bajazet / Atalide can impose no conclusion to the action. On the contrary the success of the axis of communication commanded by Roxane requires the eventual elimination of Atalide. It is envisaged that she should form another set with Acomat since part of his bargain with all of them is that Atalide will be his, an 'unnatural' set that will never materialise (and which is not dramatically explored). Once Roxane has discovered the treachery of the two lovers she believes there is a chance of rejoining the axis which includes Amurat. They are of course, as it turns out, all doomed, but we suspect that in any case Roxane's love for Bajazet has been such that she could never return to Amurat in any meaningful sense. Zatime warns Roxane:

> Et qui sait si déjà quelque bouche infidèle
> Ne l'a point averti de votre amour nouvelle? (ll. 1290–91)

Characters can of course be drawn into an axis of communication against their will. Such is the case with Hippolyte, Junie and Andromaque. Their reluctance in this context is thus another factor which contributes to the tension of utterance. Burrhus eventually realises that his prolonged inclusion in the axis of Néron, once the latter has abducted Junie, becomes more difficult to sustain. Some characters such as Eriphile are difficult to fit into any axis at all. She is the captive of Achille but has no relationship with him. Certainly she loves him, but that is never destined to be an element in negotiation between them. She never effectively engages with any other character (a sure defect in the structure of *Iphigénie*). Equally no real axis of communication exists between Pyrrhus and Oreste. Similarly, other than a simple appeal for mercy meant to move us at the moment it is made, there is no dialogue between Hermione and Andromaque, and none at all between Andromaque and Oreste.

Sometimes characters deliberately cut themselves off from axes of communication, not only because it denies the expectations of a number of characters who insist on certain things being said, but also because it can act against bringing the action to a conclusion. The most crucial case is perhaps that of Hippolyte who closes the axis of communication with his father. This means that the true nature of the situation is held back until it is too late to save Hippolyte. In the case of Phèdre it is rather that from the beginning she has no real axis of communication because any confession of love she makes to Hippolyte would be criminal. She is estranged by her love from Thésée and subsequently it is Œnone who speaks for her. Even during the meeting with Thésée in Act IV, scene 4 she is prevented from engaging with her husband once she hears the news that Hippolyte loves Aricie. Simply Phèdre has no axis of communication within which to survive. Her final isolation is her dismissal of Œnone.

Much of what I have said so far has concerned the patterning of dialogue in terms of the units, in the form of either sets or axes of communication, which determine the progress of the negotiation or transaction deriving from the project or projects which constitute the basis of the action. I should now like to turn to other aspects of the dynamics of those units at the level of dialogue. The negotiation of a project, if it is to be brought to its conclusion or completion, requires the presence of others who may not share the desire for a particular conclusion. In other words, an essential element of the dynamics of sets or axes of communication is the desire to meet or to avoid meeting. That is to say that each confrontation between the major characters is usually composed of one character who desires to see the other, the latter however not necessarily reciprocating that desire. In these circumstances, speech can only take place in an atmosphere of tension. Desire in terms of meeting conditions how characters speak to each other.[2]

The general strength of desire on the part of many characters is very clear. Jocaste wishes to bring her sons together in order to reconcile them. Bérénice wishes to see Titus in order to gain confirmation of his intention to marry her now he is no longer in mourning for the death of his father. The desire for dialogue which is shared between two characters is precisely what Néron envies in Junie and Britannicus: 'Et ce sont ces plaisirs et ces pleurs que j'envie' (659). Roxane ardently desires the presence of Bajazet and so on.

Other sets are conditioned by a positive lack of desire on the part of each interlocutor. In *Alexandre* it is clear that Porus and Taxile have little desire to meet since they love the same woman and do not share the same political aims, although they might be considered to form a natural set, both coming under the threat of defeat by Alexandre himself. Néron and Britannicus, for most of the play at least, can hardly be regarded as sharing a desire to meet. Etéocle and Polynice obviously fall into this category, as do Joad and the couple Mathan / Athalie.

By far the most interesting situations are those where one of the characters desires to meet the other but where the desire is not reciprocated. What, in these circumstances, are the patterns of desire in *Andromaque*? At their first meeting, while Oreste desires to meet Hermione, the reverse is hardly true even though Hermione attempts to convince Oreste that it is, an attempt which he soon sees through. A rather more complex situation occurs in Act IV, scene 3 when Oreste arrives after having been summoned by Hermione. Does she really desire to meet him in the same way that he desires to meet her? The terms of the mutual desire he wishes for so much quickly become a subject of doubt for him once he hears of her wish to kill Pyrrhus. Another change occurs on his return from the scene of the crime when he expects their meeting to be based on a shared desire to be with each other, but again he rapidly learns otherwise.

Similar complexities can be discerned in the relationship between Bérénice and Antiochus. What is the relationship of desire at the beginning of their first meeting in Act I, scene 4? Since Antiochus has held the status of the favoured confidant of the queen and emperor, Bérénice desires to see Antiochus as she would a friend. He, however, is about to declare his love to her, thus ressuscitating a relationship she had declared impossible five years previously. Is she really a desired interlocutor for him during that scene, given that he is certainly unsure of the reception he will get (ll. 27–30)? His express desire, however, is to clarify the situation regarding the marriage that is supposed to be taking place between Bérénice and Titus. The situation is a little more complex on the occasion of their next meeting in Act III, scene 3. Bérénice makes it quite clear that she has no desire to see him. After all, she is not aware of the need for any transaction between them. Her desire is even further diminished when she learns his news, which she refuses to believe.

The scenes between Titus and Bérénice are not without problems in this context. For example, what is the status of each interlocutor within the pattern of desire in Act IV, scene 5? Bérénice has of course asked to see Titus, presumably with the aim of persuading him to change his mind (see ll. 972–78). But it is not the same desire that has been part of their exchanges in the past. In this sense *Bérénice* helps us understand that various qualities are attached to the desire for dialogue in the plays. The status of Titus in this pattern of desire is one of ambiguity. He does not desire this meeting for he must tell her that she must leave Rome. But can he eliminate all desire to meet Bérénice? This is indeed the subject of his soliloquy in Act IV, scene 4. Act V, scene 5 almost reverses the position of their previous meeting. This time it is Titus who desires to see Bérénice whereas she resents his presence:

> Je veux partir. Pourquoi vous montrer à ma vue?
> Pourquoi venir encore aigrir mon désespoir? (ll. 1304–6)

It may well be that a change in the pattern of desire between one set of characters modifies the pattern of desire between the characters of another. In *Mithridate* the rumoured death of the king has allowed Monime and Xipharès to come together (although Monime's declaration to Xipharès is not made until after the king's return). But Xipharès's declaration has two consequences. First, Xipharès will find difficulty in facing his father. Secondly, Monime can no longer desire to see Mithridate, as she might previously have done:

> Regarde en quel état tu veux que je me montre:
> Vois ce visage en pleurs: et loin de le chercher,
> Dis-moi plutôt, dis-moi que je m'aille cacher. (ll. 388–90)

Indeed in Act IV, scene 4 it turns out that neither Monime nor Mithridate is the desired interlocutor of the other.

Not surprisingly *Phèdre*, which also involves a return, presents similar problems, especially between Hippolyte and Thésée on the one hand, and Phèdre and Thésée on the other. Both Phèdre and Hippolyte flee the king at his entrance, and this is particularly important given that they would both be the desired interlocutors of Thésée. But a particular problem emerges before this one in the course of the meeting between Phèdre and Hippolyte in Act II, scene 5. The situation with Hippolyte is quite clear. There is no way that the queen is a desired interlocutor for him. On the level of passion Hippolyte is most certainly desired by Phèdre. But is this true at the level of speech for she knows precisely how vulnerable she is to self-betrayal (a theme I shall pursue in the next chapter), having banished him once before? In fact her stated purpose in the encounter is the safety of her son. As in *Mithridate* it is her declaration which causes difficulty in the pattern of desire within dialogue, henceforth organised around Thésée. In normal circumstances, Thésée would be the desired interlocutor of his son. Hippolyte, however, cannot desire to see him in quite the same way, especially as he does not wish to reveal the truth of events. The status of each interlocutor within the pattern of desire in Act IV, scene 2 is thus problematic for both characters.

In certain sets it is necessity rather than desire which results in characters accepting to speak and to be with another. This is true of Andromaque in her meeting with Hermione for which, in contrast to the meetings with Pyrrhus that we see on stage, she takes the initiative. In Act IV, scene 2 of *Britannicus* Néron has no desire to meet with his mother: he knows all too well what her effect on him will be (see ll. 496–506). But he cannot escape seeing her. All Bajazet's meetings with Roxane are based on necessity, as is the relationship of Atalide with Roxane. In the beginning it is through necessity that Phèdre decides to meet with Hippolyte, as indeed it is a necessary courtesy for Hippolyte to meet with Phèdre, as Aricie reminds him:

> Seigneur, vous ne pouvez refuser de l'entendre.
> Quoique trop convaincu de son inimitié,
> Vous devez à ses pleurs quelque ombre de pitié.
>
> (ll. 566–68)

Finally, Phèdre's presence at the end of the play is desired only as necessary to the revelation of the truth.

It is evident that linked with the patterns of desire in dialogue is the problem of the status of the interlocutor at any given stage of the action of the play, since reflexions on status of this sort are particularly productive of anxiety among the characters. This is true of the situation of Antiochus in the scenes we have already examined. He has to ask himself: what am I to Bérénice? What gives me the right to be in her presence? Indeed, in the course of the play, he changes status from friend to enemy, especially as he becomes involved with Titus's dismissal of Bérénice. His status becomes false. The only real status that any interlocutor of Bérénice can have is that of one who is a partner to her love for Titus. In the first place he declares his own love, which she has expressly forbidden, and in the second, he associates himself with the end of her relationship with Titus. In Act V, scene 6 the latter finds himself in an uncertain status, as if the conditions of discourse had been suspended:

> Moi-même à tous moments je me souviens à peine
> Si je suis empereur, ou si je suis Romain.
> Je suis venu vers vous sans savoir mon dessein:
> Mon amour m'entraînait, et je venais peut-être
> Pour me chercher moi-même et pour me reconnaître.
>
> (ll. 1380–84)

This is important because at other stages of the action the terms of the transaction have been very clear. Titus here loses sight of the project, and, as a result, of his status as interlocutor. His voice thus becomes uncertain.

The status of a character as interlocutor may not always be clear from the very beginning. How, for example do Xipharès and Monime perceive their status in Act I, scene 2? For Monime it is certainly different from what it later becomes, since, anxious for her safety, she sees Xipharès out of necessity. Indeed it changes with Mithridate in the space of less than one Act. In Act III, scene 5 she is still a woman very much submitting to the power of Mithridate. Their next meeting in Act IV, scene 4 reverses the power relations at least at the level of dialogue. Mithridate himself is a character concerned with his own status as interlocutor. He more or less asks Arbate how he will be able to speak to his sons and to Monime:

> Mais tous deux en ces lieux que pouvaient-ils attendre?
> L'un et l'autre à la reine ont-ils osé prétendre?
> Avec qui semble-t-elle en secret s'accorder?
> Moi-même de quel œil dois-je ici l'aborder? (ll. 475–78)

In *Iphigénie* the status of the couple Iphigénie and Achille as interlocutors is never very clear. They are, as lovers promised to each other, a natural set, but they rarely operate as one. Iphigénie's agreement to the sacrifice means that Achille never really knows where he stands, especially as Clytemnestre sides with Achille against the sacrifice. Iphigénie on the other hand refuses to isolate Agamemnon as an interlocutor.

The character of Abner in *Athalie* also presents a problem. What voice can he speak with? His position is difficult in either camp, that is to say in that of Athalie and that of the Jews. He serves the queen but is prepared to defend the Jews in her presence. On the other hand, we never hear him defend Athalie or explain why he serves her. With Joad, in Act I, scene 1 he does not speak wholeheartedly as a Jew because he doubts the continuation of God's support for his people (see ll. 129–136). In fact all the time, Joad has power over Abner's status as an interlocutor because he has privileged knowledge which would help Abner clarify his status, a knowledge he refuses to divulge until the very last moment. As far as Joad himself is concerned, it is almost as if he has no human interlocutor. His communion is with God. There is certainly no negotiation as such in which he is involved with other characters. He speaks to characters rather than with them. This is brought out powerfully in Act III, scene 7 where the act of speech transcends the stage. There are no interlocutors in the same sense that there are in the profane tragedies because Joad speaks with the voice of God. No transaction is possible with God.

The major problem of characters in terms of their status within the negotiation of the transaction is the loss of interlocutors or isolation within dialogue. Simply, they 'lose' their voice, a particularly poignant aspect of their situation, especially if, as I shall claim, speech for the characters is life. This is fundamentally true of Agrippine. She has lost Néron who proceeds to banish her allies (l. 494 and ll. 811–12). With Néron's repudiation of Octavie, Agrippine witnesses the dissolution of the axis of communication I have referred to previously, perhaps an appropriate fate for one who has previously isolated Britannicus from his possible interlocutors (ll. 1144–48). Néron is the ultimate victim in that the very axis he wishes to create in opposition to his mother's disappears with the departure of Junie to the Vestal Virgins. He loses the very interlocutor who was essential to that axis.

Bérénice too gradually finds herself isolated within dialogue. At a time when she is expecting to resume communication with Titus, she loses, through an ill-judged confession on the part of Antiochus, the person she considered a special sort of confidant at a time when perhaps she needed him most. Instead of Antiochus becoming the intermediary between the queen and Titus, he involves himself as the messenger of Titus. The latter also disappears as an interlocutor, or at least appears only to affirm this disappearance. In *Bajazet* it is Atalide who finds that her lines of communication are gradually being taken away from her. The action of the play begins with the end of her role as intermediary between Bajazet and Roxane, thus immediately threatening her communication with Bajazet which that role has allowed and protracted. Her isolation is brought home to her on the news of the reconciliation of Bajazet and Roxane, news which proves to be a misinterpretation of events: 'Pourquoi de ce conseil moi seule suis-je excluse?' (l. 934) Agamemnon finds himself deprived of interlocutors from the start of the action. He has no sympathy with Ulysse or Calchas, and, having accepted the sacrifice, can speak neither to Iphigénie, nor to his wife and especially not to Achille.

Mithridate is another character who is gradually isolated in the course of the action, although, as I have remarked in an earlier discussion, this isolation does not remain permanent. He comes to the realisation that Monime and both his sons have betrayed him: 'Tout m'abandonne ailleurs, tout me trahit ici' (l. 1013) It is significant that a number of the cases of isolation within dialogue that I have discussed so far have related to characters in positions of power. Indeed one cannot terminate this discussion without some reference to *Phèdre* and in particular to Thésée. Phèdre is deprived of interlocutors first through her very attempts to communicate with Hippolyte. By its very nature her confession cannot be repeated, which rules out further meetings with him despite the encouragement she receives from Œnone. In any case the return of Thésée forecloses that option. But her confession also prevents her from communication with her husband. Her only attempt in Act IV, scene 4 is brought to an abrupt halt when she learns of the prince's love for Aricie. Hippolyte too loses Thésée as an interlocutor and, by virtue of his father's curse, the possibility of others besides Aricie;

> Chargé du crime affreux dont vous me soupçonnez,
> Quels amis me plaindront, quand vous m'abandonnez?
> (ll. 1143–44)

As far as Thésée is concerned, the whole of the fifth act constitutes an increasing isolation in speech. Aricie leaves him bewildered, as does the news of the suicide of Œnone just as he calls on her for enlightenment; he then receives the news of his son's death and, finally, Phèdre enters only to reveal the truth before she dies.

So far I have been concerned with aspects of the patterning of dialogue in the tragedies. This is seen to be organised into sets and axes of communication where the desire to meet is, in most cases, present on the part of one character. I have also described the action of Racinian tragedy in terms of a project or projects which characters wish to bring or see brought to some conclusion or completion. It is of course in the nature of drama as a whole to present us with conflict, a conflict which is considerably heightened in the case of tragedy. One paradoxical element of that conflict, however, is its possible resolution. But it is first in divergence that the tension of utterance is most obvious.[3]

Certain types of divergence are intrinsic to some relationships, especially among certain types of sets. It is obvious that divergence is at the very heart of the relationships in *La Thébaïde*. Not only is there discord between the two brothers but the role of Créon is entirely set against any agreement between them, since he himself hopes thereby to ascend to the throne. Jocaste is aware of this from the first act:

> Mais avouez, Créon, que toute votre peine
> C'est de voir que la paix rend votre attente vaine,
> Qu'elle assure à mes fils le trône où vous tendez,
> Et va rompre le piège où vous les attendez. (ll. 223–26)

Créon himself explains his motives for arranging a meeting between the two brothers:

> Je veux qu'en se voyant leurs fureurs se déploient,
> Que rappelant leur haine, au lieu de la chasser,
> Ils s'étouffent, Attale, en voulant s'embrasser. (ll. 887–90)

Discord is also evident between the two brothers in *Mithridate,* who are described as two sons 'qui ne s'accordent pas' (l. 14). The only role ascribed to Eriphile in *Iphigénie* is an interruptive one, since she seems to have no grounds of accord with any of the other characters. Religion is what separates Joad and Athalie, although it is true to say that Athalie herself has not, during her reign, been confrontational in her divergence from the beliefs of the Jews (see ll. 593–597).

Other forms of divergence emerge, either just before the beginning of the action or in the course of the action itself. The state of divergence between Agrippine and Néron has not always existed, and in the past there have been grounds for convergence between them:

> Non, non, le temps n'est plus que Néron, jeune encore,
> Me renvoyait les vœux d'une cour qui l'adore,
> Lorsqu'il se reposait sur moi de tout l'état. (ll. 91–93)

Formerly Agrippine must have seen in Burrhus an ally of some sort or, as she explains herself, she would not have entrusted him with the care of her son (ll. 144–50). Now Burrhus keeps her at the emperor's door. In the course of the action it is the turn of Burrhus to diverge from his master, a divergence he recognises in Act III, scene 2. It is not until some time into the action of *Bérénice* that the queen fully realises the extent of what now separates her from Titus, although she is in a state of divergence with Antiochus from the very first act.

Some states of divergence in the plays are, however, false and often derive from misunderstanding. Such is the case with Britannicus and Junie in Act II, scene 6, where the young prince has no knowledge of Néron's role in her dismissal of him. In Act IV, scene 2 Xipharès believes he has an enemy in the palace who has betrayed him to Mithridate. Monime has of course been responsible for this 'betrayal', but only because she has been tricked into an admission of her love by Mithridate in Act III, scene 5.

But characters rarely choose to remain in a state of divergence with others. Desire is always for shared discourse which, at certain moments, they become aware of through others. In Act III, scene 8 Néron witnesses the end of an exchange where Britannicus and Junie have been able to indulge in the shared discourse he envies. Athalie too is able to recognise the shared discourse between Joas and his 'parents' from which she is excluded and which she knows she cannot replicate with the boy.[4]

Equally, characters are aware that shared discourse is what is required of them. It is clear to all the characters in *Alexandre* that the emperor wishes to bring them into his sphere of discourse rather than to have to defeat them in battle. Axiane is acutely aware of Alexandre's intentions even after the battle has taken place:

> Je sais qu'il se dispose à me venir parler,
> Qu'en me rendant mon sceptre il veut me consoler.
> Il croit peut-être, il croit que ma haine étouffée
> A sa fausse douceur servira de trophée. (ll. 999–1002)

Pyrrhus expects Andromaque to be persuaded by his arguments in order to save her son. Bérénice expects the shared discourse of the past between her and Titus to continue. He however wishes to move to another level of shared discourse where she would recognise the legitimacy of her own dismissal:

> Rappelez bien plutôt ce cœur qui tant de fois
> M'a fait de mon devoir reconnaître la voix.
> Il en est temps. Forcez votre amour à se taire,
> Et d'un œil que la gloire et la raison éclaire
> Contemplez mon devoir dans toute sa rigueur. (ll. 1049–53)

Mithridate wishes Monime to confirm the promise of marriage that has already been made (528–46), and does not countenance opposition to the vast military enterprise he details to his sons in Act III, scene 1.[5] It is Roxane's desire to achieve and then to demand shared discourse with Bajazet.

Indeed an aspect of the tension deriving from speech rests precisely on a belief on the part of some characters, a belief which often turns out to be false, that there are grounds for convergence with others.[6] An essential element of the impact of Bérénice's reaction to Antiochus in Act I, scene 4 is that he entertains hopes of convergence, even in the course of his declaration:

> Je vois que votre cœur m'applaudit en secret,
> Je vois que l'on m'écoute avec moins de regret,

> Et que trop attentive à ce récit funeste,
> En faveur de Titus vous pardonnez le reste. (ll. 225–28)

Even Phénice sees the future possibility of convergence with Antiochus when she warns Bérénice that Titus has not yet declared his intention actually to marry her (ll. 292–96). In fact the play veers constantly from such hopes to their destruction, particularly in the case of Antiochus when he learns that the emperor will dismiss Bérénice and that Bérénice's intention is to leave Rome. The tension is all the greater for the hesitancy of the emperor himself after his interview with Bérénice in Act IV, scene 5. *Bérénice* illustrates the point that convergence with one character is dependent on divergence between others. This is particularly true of *Andromaque*, where Oreste's hopes of winning Hermione are improved by the refusal of Pyrrhus to honour the promise of marriage. Andromaque is safer all the time Pyrrhus maintains his plan to marry her. Hermione can only profit from Andromaque's refusal. This sort of desire for convergence leads to a particular tension because the success of one character's project depends on the speech of others from which they are themselves excluded and over which they have no control.

Convergence between characters may not on the other hand be immediately obvious at all levels. It is not clear, as I have observed in another context, that Xipharès and Monime share the discourse of love while certainly grounds for shared discourse exist on a political level, as the argument with Pharnace in Act I, scene 3 demonstrates. It is some time before Abner moves unconditionally into the sphere of discourse shared by Joas, Joad and Josabet. The grounds for it truly exist. Abner has after all maintained allegiance to his religion, as his very presence in the temple suggests. Joad too, despite Abner's hesitation over believing in the continuation of God's protection of the Jews, recognises his worth (ll. 67–69). The problem is that Athalie too recognises this worth and his contribution to her regime:

> Je sais que dès l'enfance élevé dans les armes,
> Abner a le cœur noble, et qu'il rend à la fois
> Ce qu'il doit à son Dieu, ce qu'il doit à ses rois. (ll. 456–58)

Athalie herself yields to conceiving the possibility of shared discourse with Joas. The sound of his voice is able to move her from hostility to pity (ll. 651–53). The divergence between them is first initiated by Joas. She renews her attempts at persuasion later in the scene, only finally to be rejected outright by the future king.

Phèdre is encouraged by Œnone to believe that shared discourse is possible between her and Hippolyte:

> Votre flamme devient une flamme ordinaire.
> Thésée en expirant vient de rompre les nœuds
> Qui faisaient tout le crime et l'horreur de vos feux.
> Hippolyte pour vous devient moins redoutable,
> Et vous pouvez le voir sans vous rendre coupable. (ll. 350–54)

At this moment Œnone and Phèdre are perhaps thinking more of the fate of Phèdre's son, but there is sufficient ambiguity in the passage I have just quoted to indicate that a different construction could be put on Œnone's exhortation. Phèdre accuses Œnone of just such a suggestion: 'Tu m'as fait entrevoir que je pouvais l'aimer' (l. 772). Even so, Phèdre persists in hoping that shared discourse with Hippolyte remains a possibility (ll. 781–85). Hippolyte at first sees grounds for shared discourse with Aricie on a level other than that of love:

> L'Attique est votre bien. Je pars, et vais pour vous
> Réunir tous les vœux partagés entre nous. (ll. 507–8)

Perhaps the most complex pattern of divergent and convergent speech is to be found in *Andromaque*, where, after all, this might be expected from the conflictual nature of the various projects in the play. Pyrrhus evokes the common enemies of himself and Andromaque in order to try and create convergence between them (l. 324).[7] After Pyrrhus's return to Hermione, Andromaque relies on the shared discourse of Hermione and the king for the success of her plea to Hermione. As far as Oreste is concerned, his hope is that, given Pyrrhus's rejection of Hermione, he might discover convergence with the princess (he has loved her in the past without that love having necessarily been reciprocated (see 473)). Even after the rebuff he eventually receives from her, Oreste persists in believing that they were on the verge of shared discourse:

> Ses yeux s'ouvraient, Pylade, elle écoutait Oreste,
> Lui parlait, le plaignait ... Un mot eût fait le reste. (ll. 745–46)

Then it is the turn of Hermione to believe that at last convergence exists between her and Pyrrhus: 'Pyrrhus revient à nous' (849), only to discover that she needs convergence with Oreste in order to carry out her revenge for Pyrrhus's final rejection of her.

In most cases, as I have indicated, the grounds for believing that shared discourse can be achieved or maintained prove false. Antiochus recognises that convergence between him and Bérénice is impossible. What is interesting is that this realisation takes place on a number of occasions. The capacity to entertain illusion has long been understood as an essential feature of Racinian characters. My emphasis is that this illusion takes place primarily at the level of dialogue: it is the illusion of characters believing themselves to be able to speak on level terms with other characters. It is all part of the drama of negotiation. Coming out of that illusion contributes to the tragic impact of the plays. Antiochus has hopes in Act I, scene 2 before meeting with Bérénice, only for them to be dashed in the next scene. But Titus's revelation that the queen must leave Rome rekindles his hopes, with some encouragement from Arsace. He hopes and despairs before his next meeting with Bérénice in Act III, scene 3. Antigone believes wrongly that Etéocle will be more flexible than his brother (ll. 551–53). Incredibly, Pyrrhus believes that what he perceives as Hermione's 'indifférence' puts them in the same position, that is to say that each has simply done his or her duty:

> Nos cœurs n'étaient point faits dépendants l'un de l'autre;
> Je suivais mon devoir, et vous cédiez au vôtre;
> Rien ne vous engageait à m'aimer en effet. (ll. 1353–55)

No character in Racine wishes to remain isolated within dialogue. Pyrrhus desperately attempts to abstract himself from one form of language — the language of love with which he could never engage with Hermione — in order to find a mutual language of indifference.

Bajazet introduces us to a type of play where the conditions of discourse are false from the very beginning and where all speech is, to a certain extent, founded on illusion. Acomat actually believes in the shared discourse of Bajazet and Roxane: 'Mais vous aimez Roxane' (l. 607). This leads to Acomat being completely misled by the 'reconciliation' between them, as it is reported by him in Act III, scene 3:

> Enfin, avec des yeux qui découvraient son âme,
> L'une a tendu la main pour gage de sa flamme;
> L'autre avec des regards éloquents, pleins d'amour,
> L'a de ses feux, Madame, assurée à son tour. (ll. 885–88)

Roxane is of course the main target of false discourse as it has been created and perpetuated by Atalide in the role of intermediary between Roxane and Bajazet. The latter reveals the extent to which speech conditions are false in the play when he relates to Atalide how on a number of occasions he has come close to revealing the truth. Only the thought of what would happen to Atalide has prevented him from doing so (ll. 743–52). But even more fundamentally, the speech conditions in *Bajazet* are false, because all the time they are speaking in the course of the action, a messenger has been despatched from the battlefield with orders to kill them all. No speech conditions in the play can in any case bring about a lasting conclusion for the characters.

The speech conditions in other plays are undermined from the beginning of the action. But this is not a flaw in the plays. It serves only to underline the importance placed on the act of negotiation itself. The success or failure of negotiation is at the centre of the drama and of tragedy. Titus's failure to confirm his marriage to Bérénice means that the discourse of both Antiochus and Bérénice is in a way suspended. For Bérénice, she cannot go backwards in time and no satisfactory speech conditions can be created for the future. A relationship with Antiochus is not an option. Agamemnon has engineered a situation where all speech in *Iphigénie* is misdirected for a considerable part of the action. Achille in particular finds it all the more difficult to orientate himself as an interlocutor for being the means by which Agamemnon has created the ambiguities and ironies in the situation. The false nature of convergence in the first three acts of the play is determined by the two senses of altar, a place for marriage or sacrifice. Like the situation in *Bajazet* there is an underlying irony which renders all the suffering in the play redundant. Eriphile turns out, like Iphigénie, to be of the blood of Helen.

Mithridate too contains features similar to those I have just discussed. Mithridate is suspicious of the motives of his sons for being in Nymphée. He is right to have such suspicions, although they are allayed in the case of Xipharès by Arbate's deliberate suppression of the information that Xipharès has intended to declare his love for Monime. From the point of Mithridate's return, Mithridate is already isolated in speech. He however clings to the idea of shared discourse with his son since he knows of his past loyalty and of his opposition to the Romans (ll. 511–14 and ll. 464–74). But his son is a rival (indeed both sons are) and his meetings with Xipharès are based even more on false convergence when he places Monime in his charge.

Are speech conditions undermined in the same way in *Phèdre*? The play begins in a similar way to *Mithridate* with a revelation of one character for another, in this instance the love of Hippolyte for Aricie. Phèdre's revelation of love for Hippolyte to Œnone and to Hippolyte himself is based on the assumption that he is the Hippolytus of legend, rather than Hippolyte who has discovered and expressed passion. Her words are thus useless in terms of possible persuasion, and this is all the more poignant for her having entertained hopes of convergence. The grounds for shared discourse simply do not exist (they have not been encouraged by her previous treatment of him). The other character for whom speech conditions are false is Thésée, but this time because of a direct lie by Œnone concerning events prior to his arrival. Because of this he sees no point of convergence with Hippolyte. But Hippolyte is also responsible for perpetuating this impression through the shame that he feels on behalf of his father. Only Phèdre's revelation at the end can restore proper speech conditions. By this time it is already too late.

What, then, are the characteristics of shared discourse which make it so attractive to those who seek to obtain, maintain or restore it? Monime well understands its attraction:

> Quoi? cher Prince, avec toi je me verrais unie?
> Et loin que ma tendresse eût exposé ta vie,
> Tu verrais ton devoir, je verrais ma vertu,
> Approuver un amour si longtemps combattu?
> Je pourrais tous les jours t'assurer que je t'aime? (ll. 1175–79)

Shared discourse thus involves in the first place legitimacy, and in the second the more personal desire for Monime to be able to repeat her expression of love for the prince. That acts of speech could be removed from danger and without tension is expressed by Britannicus:

> Quoi! je ne serai plus séparé de vos charmes?
> Quoi! même en ce moment, je puis voir sans alarmes
> Ces yeux que n'ont émus ni soupirs ni terreur
> Qui m'ont sacrifié l'empire et l'empereur! (ll. 1485–87)

Shared discourse comprises here both proximity and security. For Junie shared discourse is hearing of the love she feels for Britannicus:

> Je ne vous nierai point, Seigneur, que ses soupirs
> M'ont daigné quelquefois expliquer ses désirs. (ll. 553–54)

That is the sort of situation in which Néron wishes to replace Britannicus. Bajazet, regards shared discourse as offering relief where he could: 'Chercher quelque secours contre tous mes remords' (l. 1000). For Agrippine it represents the restoration of the past when her orders could assemble the senate and when she was its 'âme toute-puissante' (l. 96). Shared discourse for her is more one-sided: it involves rather acquiescence on the part of others (she is a profane sort of Joad in fact).

What of *Andromaque* or indeed of other plays where love and power combine to encourage or enforce a form of convergence? *Andromaque* is interesting because it is one of only two plays where this situation ends in success for the character who possesses power (the other is *Mithridate*). Pyrrhus's conditions for convergence are straightforward: 'Sauvez-le, sauvez-nous' (l. 960). Hitherto Andromaque has refused to yield to Pyrrhus's blackmail but she is eventually forced to realise that marriage to Pyrrhus is Astyanax's sole chance of survival and goes to see Pyrrhus in order to ensure it (Céphise reports the results of this meeting in lines 1053–63). What is interesting in Andromaque's response to having acted in this way are the grounds on which she bases her justification of this new-found 'convergence':

> Pyrrhus en m'épousant s'en déclare l'appui;
> Il suffit: je veux bien m'en reposer sur lui.
> Je sais quel est Pyrrhus: violent, mais sincère,
> Céphise, il fera plus qu'il n'a promis de faire. (ll. 1083–86)

Shared discourse can therefore involve a trust which transcends personal difference, although, ironically, such 'convergence' disguises divergence in this case.

Discussion in this chapter has been directed towards laying the foundation for more particular and detailed analyses of the importance of acts of speech and their contribution to the tragic action. The patterning of dialogue in the way I have described it underpins the relationships — desired or otherwise — which bring characters together in speech. The emphasis I have placed on the notion of sets and axes of communication also generates the expectation so important to the way characters speak and listen. It is what they hear and say — and their manner of speaking and listening — which determines fulfilment or denial of that expectation. Convergent or divergent discourse will be important in my discussion of substitution, that is to say where characters in certain cases speak for others. Both concepts contribute in addition to expectation which projects discourse into the future, into a 'speech' future.

In any case, acts of speech, whatever their poetic quality, do not in themselves generate tragedy. This is the result of a careful and well-prepared structuring of the dialogue. In addition, the general conditions of speech, where the meetings of the characters are managed and where the moves of one character towards or away from another, must be such that they can bear the weight of passion that is placed upon them. It is only then that the tension of utterance can be at its most effective. The tension of utterance is what I should now like to explore in its various manifestations.

Chapter 2
Theatre and Speech

The general conditions of speech which were the subject of the previous chapter, where I emphasised the importance of the patterning of dialogue in particular, demonstrate that Racinian dialogue does not take place in a void but is part of a *situation*. In this chapter, we shall see how the characters show themselves to be aware of who they are talking to, what position they occupy in relation to their interlocutors and the effect that has on the way they speak. Clearly the characters' speech will also be determined by the importance of the issue they are 'talking out'. But my argument here is that their speech behaviour is of crucial importance — after all they are all aware of the importance of *what* they have to say. Tragic effect will be seen to derive either from the fact of having uttered something at all, or from the way in which it has been uttered. It is often on the basis of how characters speak that they are judged, because hearing or, more particularly, a way of listening can be a form of judgement. This chapter is very much therefore about how characters negotiate each act of speech at the moment it is spoken or heard. In a sense I shall be exploring the 'existential' basis of the patterns of dialogue which provide the framework and the general structure of the plays.

The importance of acts of speech in Racinian tragedy can first be understood in the way they transform place into something special. Speech often defines in some way the quality of the place where the action occurs. Speech invests place with a special meaning by virtue of its happening there. Not the least function of the relation between speech and location is that it sets up an expectation of what is to be said. Antiochus thus describes the setting of *Bérénice*:

> Souvent ce cabinet superbe et solitaire
> Des secrets de Titus est le dépositaire.
> C'est ici quelquefois qu'il se cache à sa cour,
> Lorsqu'il vient à la reine expliquer son amour. (ll. 3-4)

At various moments in the play we are reminded that this particular room is inseparable from the idea of explanation. It is a question of here and nowhere else. Bérénice expects to see Titus there for a specific purpose:

> Il va sur tant d'états couronner Bérénice,
> Pour joindre à plus de noms le nom d'impératrice.
> Il m'en viendra lui-même assurer en ce lieu. (ll. 175-77)

Bérénice later emphasises to Titus: 'Moi-même j'ai voulu vous entendre en ce lieu' (l. 1109).[1] Antiochus cannot stand any longer hearing the name of Titus pronounced by Bérénice (ll. 275-76) in the place where he has himself conversed as a friend with the emperor and the queen. The reason Titus sends Antiochus to tell Bérénice that she must leave is in order to spare him from sharing with her once again the space which has heard words of an entirely different nature. Removing a quality of speech deprives the space of its meaning.

The special relation of place to speech is a major feature of *Bajazet.* Acomat looks forward to the appearance of Roxane in the harem: 'La sultane en ce lieu se doit rendre' (l. 1). The speech that now occurs in the harem is marked as exceptional by Osmin who remarks that previously access to this place was forbidden them (ll. 3-5). The harem is in other words transformed by the nature of the speech which it now hears. In fact *Bajazet* illustrates the dual taboo composed of a forbidden place and forbidden words. This is what makes appearance in such a place so vulnerable, as Bajazet himself realises in the case of Roxane:

> Vous ne craigniez rien tant que d'être refusée;
> Que même mes refus vous auraient exposée;
> Qu'après avoir osé me voir et me parler,
> Il était dangereux pour vous de reculer. (ll. 1510-13)

Once movement into this location has occurred there is no retreat from it, as there can be no retreat from the words spoken within it.

As some of these examples therefore imply, the place represented by the stage itself is qualitatively different from other sorts of space mentioned in the text, however important these may be in the overall space represented at the level of the imagination alone, what Maskell calls 'geographic space' (p.18). The stage in *Britannicus* is where Néron, apart from one scene where he apparently reverts to the previous relationship with his mother, attempts to establish his own voice, particularly in his relationship with Junie. It is very different from the Senate where, from behind a veil, Agrippine has been the real controlling voice (ll. 91-98). Junie is certainly aware that her enforced translation from one place to another is related to a different type of language because she hears Néron declare his love for her and invite her to be his empress:

> Et pouvez-vous, Seigneur, souhaiter qu'une fille
> Qui vit presque en naissant éteindre sa famille,
> Qui dans l'obscurité nourissant sa douleur,
> S'est fait une vertu conforme à son malheur,

Passe subitement de cette nuit profonde
Dans un rang qui l'expose à tout le monde,
Dont je n'ai pu de loin soutenir la clarté,
Et dont une autre enfin remplit la majesté? (ll. 611-18)

Junie is later permitted to escape from the place represented by the stage to the temple of the Vestal Virgins where she may find refuge in silence (she has lost her most important interlocutor in Britannicus).[2]

The significance of moving from one place to another and the role speech plays in determining the quality of the space is emphasized in this speech of Junie's by the reference to exposure to light. The theme of light and obscurity is obviously sustained on a much more poetic level in *Phèdre* but it takes on its full significance only in relation to speech. As with Junie, the move from obscurity (Junie has stayed clear of the splendour of the court: 'Elle se dérobait même à sa renommée' (l. 416)) is associated with the unwelcome need to speak and to listen. Phèdre leaves her darkened room for the light where she will enunciate what should never have been spoken or heard. Speech transforms place and sullies the light. Ironically she expresses the desire to rest 'à l'ombre des forêts' (l. 176). The forest is a place of shade and non-speech. That place loses its significance when the sort of speech previously associated with it ceases is further illustrated when Théramène points out to Hippolyte that: 'Les forêts de nos cris moins souvent retentissent' (l. 133). Hippolyte emerges from the forest to declare himself to Aricie in a 'foreign' language and hears Phèdre make her infamous declaration. A different form of obscurity is mentioned in *Iphigénie.* Agamemnon complains that fame has exposed him to the fatality of having to make a terrible promise to the gods:

Heureux qui, satisfait de son humble fortune,
Libre du joug superbe où je suis attaché,
Vit dans l'état obscur où les dieux l'ont caché. (ll. 10-12)

Eriphile too moves from obscurity to a form of exposure although the connection with speech is less well marked.

There is however a more fundamental way in which speech relates to place. In order for the negotiation to be completed characters need to meet as a necessity. Presence is therefore a demand, especially within the context of power which is at the centre of many relationships, the relationship of necessity I discussed in the previous chapter. The act of speech cannot be enunciated 'in the wings' so to speak, nor can it be enunciated by a third party, as we shall see in the next chapter. This presence is moreover enhanced by the expectation which underpins all meetings between major characters in the plays and which is determined by the specific nature of the issue at hand. The place represented by the stage is thus fundamentally a place of presence, but a presence inseparable from speech.[3] The emotional impact of this form of presence is that each time the characters see each other their meeting is consequential. Much is therefore invested in every single confrontation, all the more so because the characters do not meet often. The baseline of every meeting is that things *must* be said, even if it turns out that their utterance is deferred. In this sense the relationship between the visual and the vocal is an *imperative* one.

At one level the imperative nature of the relationship between presence and speech can be perceived in the explicit demand made by some characters of others. Esther specifically requires the presence of Aman in order to 'rompre ce grand silence' (ll. 696-97). Agrippine spends much of her time in the play demanding to see Néron and is unwilling to move: 'Je veux l'attendre ici' (l. 7). This contrasts with a previous stage in her relationship with her son. Gone are the days when:

> [...] derrière un voile, invisible et présente,
> J'étais de ce grand corps l'âme toute puissante. (ll. 95-6)

On other occasions the demand of presence is determined more by the need for particular explanations or revelations to be given or made. Bérénice expects the appearance of Titus in the antechamber, their usual meeting-place. Agamemnon needs the presence of his daughter for the continuation of his mission to Troy. Moreover, the characters often know that certain encounters are inescapable. The situation commands their mutual presence in the same place at the same time. The imperative nature of the relationship is sometimes articulated in the orders some characters give to others. Britannicus urges Narcisse: 'Examine leurs yeux, observe leurs discours' (l. 349). Roxane tells Zatime: 'Mais au moins observez ses regards, ses discours' (l.1207).[4]

At another level this relationship appears in the frequent collocation of *voir / parler*. Bérénice underlines the intention of seeing in order to speak: 'Allons le voir: je veux lui parler tout à l'heure' (l. 912). Athalie exclaims: 'Laissez-moi, cher Mathan, le voir, l'interroger' (l. 614). Here the two verbs have equal weight in the line, but the second is almost a necessary predicate of the other.[5] That presence on the stage inevitably entails speech is a matter of concern for Titus: 'Il faut la voir, Paulin, et rompre le silence' (l. 484). Frequently, the combination of presence and speech is further marked by the use of 'bouche', 'visage' and 'yeux'. Roxane, insisting on more decisive evidence of Bajazet's love, demands:

> Je veux que devant moi sa bouche et son visage
> Me découvrent son cœur sans me laisser d'ombrage. (ll. 329-30)

Similarly, Bérénice must hear Titus himself dismiss her from his presence:

> J'attendais pour vous croire,
> Que cette même bouche, après mille serments
> D'un amour qui devait unir tous nos moments,
> Cette bouche à mes yeux s'avouant infidèle,
> M'ordonnât elle-même une absence éternelle. (ll. 1104-8)

The play on absence and presence here requires no additional comment. Titus himself knows, in advance of the scene in which Bérénice utters these words, what her requirements will be and prefigures her use of language:

> Et même en ce moment, inquiète, empressée,
> Elle veut qu'à ses yeux, j'explique ma pensée. (ll. 739-40)

The pressures of presence and speech are thus keenly felt by the characters. Iphigénie is full of foreboding at Achille's seeming reluctance to appear before her:

> Lui seul ne paraît point. Le triste Agamemnon
> Semble craindre à mes yeux de prononcer son nom. (ll. 611-12)

The most tragic — and ironic — example of this sort is undoubtedly that of Phèdre: 'J'ai déclaré ma honte aux yeux de mon vainqueur' (l. 767) This declaration was not however demanded in the same way as the others I have illustrated. In this case the physical presence of Hippolyte was enough to provoke speech welcomed by neither the prince nor Phèdre. This example reaffirms nonetheless the ineluctable relationship of presence and speech. It is impossible to escape from it.

The fact that presence is a necessary concomitant of speech is recognised by Racine in the way that the demands of presence are matched by the characters' desire to avoid it. Néron has a special reason to avoid Agrippine's presence: 'Eloigné de ses yeux, j'ordonne, je menace' (l.496). He is unable to sustain this level of authority when he is with her (l.506):

> Et c'est pour m'affranchir de cette dépendance,
> Que je la fuis partout, [...] (ll. 507-8)

The two plays which involve the return of a character who has been reported dead are particularly significant in this regard. In *Mithridate* Monime, having heard with pleasure the declaration of Xipharès, cannot possibly go to meet the king:

> Vois ce visage en pleurs; et loin de le chercher,
> Dis-moi plutôt, dis-moi que je m'aille cacher. (ll. 389-90)

Characters cannot wait to disappear once Thésée has returned, something which alerts him to the trouble that awaits:

> Que vois-je? Quelle horreur dans ces lieux répandue
> Fait fuir devant mes yeux ma famille éperdue? (ll. 953-54)

Before this it has been noted that Hippolyte has avoided the presence of Aricie (ll. 404-5). It is with good reason too that Titus wishes to stay away from Bérénice, because he knows exactly what he must say to her:

> Epargnez à mon cœur cet éclaircissement.
> Allez, expliquez-lui mon trouble et mon silence:
> Surtout qu'elle me laisse éviter sa présence. (ll. 741-43)

This is especially so given that the lives of the two characters have been bound up with speech and that they have met each other every day for five years.

The structure of presence and absence with regard to speech is also at the centre of the tragic situation of *Iphigénie*. Eriphile for example wishes to escape the presence of Achille because she cannot explain publicly her desire for him (ll. 889-92). Indeed the play begins with Agamemnon's order to Arcas to intercept Clytemnestre and her daughter in order to prevent them from arriving in Aulis so that Agamemnon too can avoid explanation. After it has been revealed that Iphigénie is to be sacrificed Agamemnon again attempts to avoid seeing his wife, as she herself notes:

> Agamemnon m'évite, et craignant mon visage,
> Il me fait de l'autel refuser le passage. (ll. 1045-46)

Like Thésée, Iphigénie notices the reluctance of her father to greet her properly:

> Seigneur, où courez-vous? et quels empressements
> Vous dérobent sitôt à nos embrassements? (ll. 531-32)

The link between seeing and speaking is such in Racine that failure or reluctance to speak must always be explained.

But such are the pressures of speech that attempts at avoidance are futile. At no point is this more poignant than in Hippolyte's admission to Aricie: 'Présente je vous fuis, absente je vous trouve' (l. 542). Agrippine is quite adamant that Néron's flight will be to no avail:

> Le coupable Néron fuit en vain ma colère:
> Tôt ou tard il faudra qu'il entende sa mère. (ll. 919-20)

In fact his deliberate absence is a spur to her pursuit: 'Mais je le poursuivrai d'autant plus qu'il m'évite' (l. 123). Agamemnon has expressed the desire that he should be spared the screams 'd'une mère en fureur' (l. 147). In Act IV, scene 4 they catch up with him: 'Voilà, voilà les cris que je craignais d'entendre' (l. 1314). For Antiochus it is avoidance that comes too late:

> J'évite, mais trop tard,
> Ces cruels entretiens où je n'ai point de part. (ll. 273-74)

Or it is countered by obligation. Hippolyte is reluctant to see Phèdre in Act II, scene 5 but is reminded of his position by Aricie: 'Seigneur, vous ne pouvez refuser de l'entendre' (l. 566). In Act II, scene 4 Hippolyte asks Théramène to return in order to deliver him from 'un fâcheux entretien' (ll. 579-80). Théramène fails to return in time.

The dynamics of Racinian tragedy are, as I have shown, determined by the demands of presence and the imperative relationship of seeing and speaking. It is however the case that characters experience difficulty in speaking and here we witness the tension of utterance at its most acute. In the first place the expectation set up both by the specific nature of the transaction and the demands of presence as speech are denied. Titus meets Bérénice in Act II, scene 4 but fails to deliver the speech that she expects.[6] Bajazet confronts Roxane for the first time without help from Atalide, and is unable to satisfy her expectation in terms of what she has been led to believe. His 'aphasia', as Barthes describes it,[7] is marked in a simple aside: 'O ciel! que ne puis-je parler?' (l. 560) Failure to speak is thus as much an event as speaking, certainly in the sense that the consequences of that failure can be a matter of life or death, as Hippolyte also discovers. Phèdre is unable even to name Hippolyte (ll. 260-62). Andromaque fails to complete a single sentence of the message that Céphise must take to Pyrrhus (l. 1039 and l. 1043). Titus refers to his general inability to utter what is required in particular circumstances:

> Vingt fois depuis huit jours
> J'ai voulu devant elle en ouvrir le discours;
> Et dès le premier mot ma langue embarrassée
> Dans ma bouche vingt fois a demeuré glacée. (ll. 473-76)

Instances like these illustrate the degree to which Racinian characters are vulnerable through their speech. Speaking or failing to speak is what eventually undoes them, as we shall observe on many occasions.

The fierce resentment of absence and silence in Racine's tragedies which is often a source of impatience is illustrated by the frequent use of the imperative forms of the verbs of speaking and saying. *Bérénice* offers excellent examples of this phenomenon. Titus demands that Paulin tell him exactly what the Romans think of his intended marriage: 'Parlez donc. Que faut-il que Bérénice espère?' (l. 367) The imperative becomes more urgent in the mouth of Bérénice herself. She can wait no longer for Antiochus to express himself unambiguously: 'Que craignez-vous? Parlez: c'est trop longtemps se taire' (l. 183) When the language of Titus breaks down during their first meeting, the simple 'Parlez' is full of significance. Again Bérénice's impatience emerges during the second meeting between her and Titus when he himself explains why she must leave Rome. His explanation is clearly insufficient:

> Rome a ses droits, Seigneur: n'avez-vous pas les vôtres?
> Ses intérêts sont-ils plus sacrés que les nôtres?
> Dites, parlez. (ll. 1151-53)

The imperative form is not a line filler. It commands characters, especially in its status as a marker of power, to act in a way they are most reluctant to act, or in a way they find most difficult.

The tension of utterance which is a sign of the problems I have mentioned so far undoubtedly derives its importance from the momentous nature of what must be said, sometimes in response to the imperative form of verbs of speaking and saying, even in the case of minor figures. As Acomat warns Osmin:

> Songe que du récit, Osmin, que tu vas faire
> Dépendent les destins de l'empire ottoman. (ll. 14-15)

Antiochus realises only too well the import of the message he must now impart from Titus to Bérénice: 'Je n'ai qu'à vous parler pour me faire haïr' (l. 882). Nowhere is this more important than in the case of Phèdre who is more than conscious of the nature of her confession to Hippolyte. It is sixteen lines after Œnone's 'Parlez: je vous écoute' (l. 246) before

Phèdre finally confesses. Her horror at what she must say is marked immediately by her exclamation: 'Ciel! que lui vais-je dire?' (l. 247). Even before this point Phèdre feels that she can proceed no further:

> Je t'en ai dit assez. Epargne-moi le reste.
> Je meurs pour ne point faire un aveu si funeste. (ll. 225-26)

Once she has confessed she again refers to her 'aveu', describing it this time as 'honteux' (l. 694).[8]

The importance of what the characters have to impart to others serves to underline the difficulty of utterance at the moment of its production. Again the word 'parler' carries with it a weight peculiar to Racinian tragedy. All the responsibility of speech is encapsulated in Œnone's offer to speak to Thésée for Phèdre: 'Je parlerai' (l. 899). The isolation of this locution in the line stands almost equal in importance to 'J'aime'. Arcas is aware of the importance of utterance at the moment of revealing the true destiny of Iphigénie:

> Dût tout cet appareil retomber sur ma tête,
> Il faut parler. (ll. 906-7)

Bérénice is particularly rich in the articulation of the difficulties of articulation. An awareness of the importance of utterance is exhibited by Titus: 'Voici le temps enfin qu'il faut que je m'explique' (l. 343). Titus cannot even complete the sentence containing the words of dismissal he must say: 'Je vais, Paulin ... O ciel! puis-je le déclarer?' (l. 445) Other terms also indicate the degree to which the need to speak weighs heavily on the characters. It is understandable that Titus should offer a further example: 'Quelle nouvelle, ô ciel! je lui vais annoncer!' (l. 549) On two occasions Titus actually enunciates alone what he must later say to Bérénice herself, while at the same time asking himself whether he will manage to do so. The first is in Act II, scene 3 (ll. 521-22). The second occurs in his soliloquy immediately prior to his meeting with Bérénice in Act IV, scene 5: 'Pourrai-je dire enfin: "Je ne veux plus vous voir"' (l. 998).

One particular problem in speaking, the public exposure constituted by language, is demonstrated by the relatively wide distribution at crucial moments of the plays of Racine's use of 'prononcer', where the senses of vocal articulation and public pronouncement unite in a powerful way. Pyrrhus is forced to confront the full horror of his order to kill Astyanax by Andromaque's question: 'Et vous prononcerez un arrêt si cruel?' (l. 275) Agamemnon is all too aware of the nature of his order to sacrifice his daughter: 'Puis-je leur prononcer cet ordre sanguinaire ?' (l. 1430)

The vocal aspects of the term are made more obvious in *Bajazet.* First Bajazet *writes* to Atalide that, as far as Roxane is concerned:

> ni la mort, ni vous-même,
> Ne me ferez jamais prononcer que je l'aime. (ll. 1142-43)

Secondly, Roxane finally realizes in her last meeting with Bajazet: 'Tu ne sauras jamais prononcer que tu m'aimes' (l. 1306-7). In other words she will never hear it. There are times however when public declarations can be helpful. They are significant in their rarity. Andromaque has more confidence in Pyrrhus's promise of protection for her son because of his having publicly declared it (ll. 1083-84), and Mardochée considers that only Esther's declaration that she is a Jew (her identity has hitherto been kept a secret) can save her people from extinction (ll. 189-90).

The concentration one finds on the difficulties of articulation in Racinian tragedy, the emphasis on commands to voice thoughts and the place of speech requiring the physical presence of characters all point to the physical dimension of speech itself. This can often be obscured by the view of Racine's plays as representing a world of transcendance where the abstract supposedly has precedence over the physical.[9] Indeed the view that part of the dramatic intention is to draw our attention to this dimension is supported by the number of times the word 'bouche' occurs in Racinian tragedy (sixty-three times in fact — and not once in *Les Plaideurs*). The physical reference contained in the reference to 'bouche' is well illustrated by Junie who, on Néron's orders, will have to inform Britannicus that he can no longer aspire to her love:

> Moi! que je lui prononce un arrêt si sévère?
> Ma bouche mille fois lui jura le contraire. (ll. 675-76)

Bajazet's inability to voice words of love to Roxane is accentuated by his reaction to Atalide's belief that he has done just that:

> Ah! croyez-vous que, loin de le penser,
> Ma bouche seulement eût pu le prononcer? (ll. 979-80)

Such a declaration would be a form of blasphemy (the very term derives from the notion of speech). The end of utterance is the context in which 'bouche' appears in *Britannicus.* Agrippine complains: 'Ah! l'on s'efforce en vain de me fermer la bouche' (ll. 832-33). Since the main axis of communication has hitherto been formed by Néron and his mother whose constant presence has largely determined the progress of that axis, Néron's (and Narcisse's) attempts to remove Agrippine from his sphere of influence are attempts to separate them physically. After all it is when he is far from his mother that Néron can speak independently, an independence which disintegrates whenever he is reunited with her. She is excluded from the stage and is thus reduced to silence. As far as Phèdre is concerned, it is a question of her body attempting one thing while her mind can only succeed in the contrary:

> Quand ma bouche implorait le nom de la déesse,
> J'adorais Hippolyte [...] (ll. 285-86)

It is no coincidence that *Phèdre* is one tragedy which foregrounds above all others the suffering of the body. Indeed physical suffering is sometimes direcly connected with the act of speaking in the plays. Arsace describes Antiochus as: 'Tremblant d'avoir osé s'expliquer devant elle' (l. 783). Antiochus had already anticipated the effects of speaking in the first scene of the play:

> Mais quoi? déjà je tremble, et mon cœur agité
> Craint autant ce moment que je l'ai souhaité. (ll. 21-22)

Hippolyte experiences the same sensation before his father: 'Je venais en tremblant vous le dire à vous-même' (l. 1130).

So far I have concentrated on the problems involved in the context of utterance and in aspects of the utterance itself. The tension of utterance is of course enhanced by the characters' expression of the consequentiality of what they have to say. Things would not be so bad if they could be said and then forgotten. Unfortunately it turns out that the full consequences of the characters' utterances are not immediately apparent at the time of speaking. Phèdre, Monime and Xipharès all discover this sad fact.

The actual consequences of speaking make a great impact on the characters. Monime knows what she has done in revealing her love for Xipharès and also knows what is likely to happen:

> Que dis-je? quand peut-être il y va de ta vie,
> Je parle. (ll. 1144-45)

Speech is therefore a matter of life or death. Roxane is brutally clear on this point: 'Sa perte ou son salut dépend de sa réponse' (l. 326). Certain conditions may in themselves lead to unfortunate consequences. Esther, on being urged by Mardochée to go and reveal her identity to Assuérus in order to save the Jews from the command to exterminate them, tells him that the very act of speaking in his presence without permission is fatal:

> Et la mort est le prix de tout audacieux
> Qui sans être appelé se présente à leurs yeux (i.e. les rois).
> (ll. 195-96)

Equally dangerous, however, are the consequences of refusal to speak. Roxane makes these quite clear for Bajazet:

> Et sans ce même amour qu'offensent vos refus
> Songez-vous, en un mot, que vous ne seriez plus?
> (ll. 511-12)

Néron warns Junie against: 'La gloire d'un refus sujet au repentir' (l. 626). But, apart perhaps from Bajazet, the perils of failing to speak are the greatest in the case of Hippolyte, as Aricie impresses upon him: 'Quoi! vous pouvez vous taire en ce péril extrême?' (l. 1329) Hippolyte has already explained his silence to Thésée:

> D'un mensonge si noir justement irrité,
> Je devrais faire ici parler la vérité,
> Seigneur; mais je supprime un secret qui vous touche,
> Approuvez le respect qui me ferme la bouche. (ll. 1087-90)

The refusal to speak or to say what is required seems almost perverse in that what needs to be said amounts often to very little. Pyrrhus explains to Andromaque: 'Madame, dites-moi seulement que j'espère' (l. 325). He is thus unable to comprehend her refusal to accept his offer of sparing the life of her son: 'vous ne l'avez pas seulement demandé' (l. 910). Indeed the minimal response that is sought, usually by those characters who wield some sort of power, is seen as unproblematic, as Néron implies to Junie: 'Je vous réponds de tout; consentez seulement' (l. 622). But in other cases it is love which demands even the slightest response. Xipharès asks for 'un mot' from Monime (l. 220). Atalide urges upon Bajazet that his situation would be improved by 'un mot un peu plus doux' (l. 776).

In the case of Bérénice a simple word would be of so much consolation:

> Ce cœur après huit jours, n'a-t-il rien à me dire?
> Qu'un mot va rassurer mes timides esprits! (ll. 580-81)

Or again:

> Un soupir, un regard, un mot de votre bouche,
> Voilà l'ambition d'un cœur comme le mien. (ll. 576-77)

Oreste deceives himself into thinking that Hermione had begun at last to listen to him and that he was on the point of persuading her to leave with him: 'Un mot eût fait le reste' (746). One word from Andromaque was all that was necessary for Pyrrhus:

> Pyrrhus vous l'a promis. Vous venez de l'entendre,
> Madame: il n'attendait qu'un mot pour vous le rendre.
> (ll. 1053-54)

The concept of minimal response is productive of tension on a variety of levels. As Louis Van Delft comments: 'A single word commits a person's whole being as well as his future. The destiny of each protagonist rests upon an elementary acceptance or refusal'.[10] At the same time, as the constant exhortations to speech on the part of some characters suggest, the minimal response is delayed or even not forthcoming at all. The importance attached to this minimal response and the difficulties it seems to entail derive from the fact that much hangs on it. For Esther the survival of the Jewish people depends on a word from the mouth of Assuérus (ll. 689-90). Antiochus urges Titus to save Bérénice from her intended suicide: 'Dites un mot' (l. 1239). Acomat tells Bajazet: 'Dites un mot, et vous nous sauvez tous' (l. 620). Obviously such expressions are good examples of one form of exaggeration.[11] But this seems much closer to reality than the hyperbole of 'cent fois' and 'mille fois'. In *Bajazet* minimal utterance literally amounts to one word. Roxane warns Bajazet: 'S'il m'échappait un mot, c'est fait de votre vie' (l. 542). That word is 'Sortez' (l. 1565). Is this what Racine meant when he argued in his preface to *Bérénice* that the secret of tragedy is to 'faire quelque chose de rien'?

On the other hand characters can say too much. The tension of utterance often leads to a loss of control over language which at times takes on a momentum of its own and reveals yet again insecurity and vulnerability in the very act of communication. That language escapes the control of the speaker is obvious from the remorse characters feel at having spoken at all. In Monime's case it is a question of repeating what she has already said, but in the wrong circumstances. Having declared her love for Xipharès, she finds it all too easy to reiterate it, thus suggesting that it is better never to have spoken at all:

> Les dieux qui m'inspiraient, et que j'ai mal suivis,
> M'ont fait taire trois fois par de secrets avis.
> J'ai dû continuer. (ll. 1237-39)

In other words: 'Il fallait tout nier' (l. 1134). This is however another form of illusion.

Characters sometimes interrupt themselves in the recognition that they have gone further than they intended. In Act II, scene 1 of *Bajazet*, Roxane perceives that the discourse of power is dominating too soon the discourse of love. Having threatened Bajazet with her power to put him to death she stops momentarily in order to continue in a more conciliatory tone: 'Bajazet, écoutez: je sens que je vous aime' (l. 537). The irritation Acomat feels at Bajazet's sense of morality leads him to go further than he should with a person of superior rank: 'Je m'emporte, Seigneur ... ' (l. 651) The control with which Agrippine conducts her famous narrative of Roman history threatens to erupt into unhelpful accusations directed against Sénèque and Burrhus until she breaks off to resume her proper chain of thought (l. 1156).

The momentum of language can be such that it prevents necessary explanations from being given. In Act III, scene 7 of *Britannicus* the young prince launches into accusations against Junie's infidelity, thus wasting the precious time they have together until Narcisse can summon Néron. Junie has to interrupt him twice (l. 989 and l. 998) before she is able to give her side of the story. Indulgence in language is also perceived as fateful. Monime senses that the joy she experiences in speaking to Xipharès annuls the effect of having persuaded him that they must never see each other again:

> Plus je vous parle, et plus, trop faible que je suis,
> Je cherche à prolonger le péril que je fuis. (ll. 741-42)

Language certainly runs away with Pyrrhus in Act II, scene 5 of *Andromaque* when he appears obsessed with the thought of Andromaque after having congratulated himself on his triumph over the hold she has had on him. Phœnix realises the consequences of the king's constant references to her: 'Commencez donc, Seigneur, à ne m'en parler plus' (l. 664). Pyrrhus insists: 'Non, je n'ai pas bien dit tout ce qu'il faut lui dire' (l. 674). Racine's characters are sometimes inhabited by a compulsion to speak which eventually leads to their downfall.

Phèdre is the culmination in Racine of the depiction of this tendency. The lack of control she exhibits over her language is evident in the meeting with Hippolyte in Act II. Her revelation to Œnone in Act I is also crucial in this regard but there Œnone is pressing Phèdre to unbare her soul. In Act II Phèdre has to make a conscious effort to restrain herself before Hippolyte because she must plead for the safety of her son. The very sight of Hippolyte leads her to confuse him with Thésée and eventually to declare her love. Her loss of control is complete in her reaction to Hippolyte's apparent disingenuousness: 'Eh bien! connais donc Phèdre dans toute sa fureur' (l. 672). Interestingly, of course, Hippolyte had already lost control of his own language in his meeting with Aricie: 'Je me suis engagé trop avant' (l. 521).

The tension of utterance at the root of the characters' compulsion to speak is often the result of a form of violence from within and is a feature of the production of speech itself, even with characters whom we do not associate with other forms of violence. Xipharès can restrain his speech no longer: 'Mais enfin à mon tour, je prétends éclater' (l. 98). Pyrrhus's love for Andromaque is described in the same way: 'Pour la veuve d'Hector ses feux ont éclaté' (l. 108). Oreste admits that: ' [...] les feux mal couverts n'en éclatent que mieux' (l. 575). 'Eclater' illustrates the way that speech bursts upon the world and may indeed lead to the disintegration of the character who utters it. It marks an end to restraint and perhaps constraint, barriers which, in Racinian tragedy, can only be crossed one way.

The violence of 'éclater' is matched by 'arracher' which can also be self-induced, as with Eriphile: 'Mais mon cœur trop pressé m'arrache ce discours' (l. 479). 'Arracher' is thus associated with the momentum of speech. Or, most frequently, it is induced by others. Monime is aware that seeing Xipharès again will lead her to speak as she should not: 'Il viendra malgré moi m'arracher cet aveu' (l. 417). She later explains to Xipharès that his presence: 'Peut m'arracher du cœur quelque indigne soupir' (l. 730). Antiochus refers to the occasion on which Bérénice swore him to silence as: 'Lorsque vous m'arrachiez cette injuste promesse' (l. 207). Even Atalide regards herself as guilty of such violence in: '[...] arrachant malgré lui (= Bajazet) des gages de sa foi' (l. 1604). The most obvious link of provoking speech from a position of power is unquestionably to be found in *Mithridate*, when Monime complains of 'cet aveu honteux, où vous m'avez forcée' (l. 1347).

The pressures of provocation and violence the characters are subject to emerge most forcefully in the temptation to say more than they mean to. The risk they run is therefore self-betrayal in speech. Monime's explanation for her error of judgement in revealing her love for Xipharès to the king is that Mithridate caught her off guard (ll. 1231-32), thus suggesting that vigilance over language is a *sine qua non* of Racinian drama. The tragedy of the characters is that vigilance over language is beyond them. Self-betrayal is of course a function of the restraint and constraints I have just mentioned. In some of the tragedies it provides the mainspring of the action as a whole, as for example in *Mithridate* and *Phèdre*.

That self-betrayal is to the forefront of the experience of Racinian characters is sometimes indicated again by the playwright's use of *interruptio.*[12] Oreste, before his appearance in Act III, scene 2, has already planned to abduct Hermione and now attempts to manifest his indifference to the marriage that Pyrrhus has proposed to her. There is one moment, however, when his guard is just about to slip. Hermione comments on what she was prepared to do for Oreste who is momentarily shaken by her hypocrisy: 'Ah! que vous saviez bien cruelle ... ' (l. 825) He reverts almost immediately to a calmer form of speech. Two similar moments occur in *Mithridate,* one more crucial than the other. Monime's temptation to respond positively to Xipharès' declaration of love is marked simply by her wistful 'Prince ... ' (l. 210), whereupon she interrupts herself just in time. More dangerously, Xipharès just prevents himself from revealing to his father the real reason for his departure from Nymphée:

> Trop heureux d'avancer la fin de ma misère,
> J'irai ... J'effacerai le crime de ma mère. (ll. 939-40)

Aricie almost fails to obey Hippolyte's injunction not to reveal to Thésée the awful secret of what has transpired in Trézène:

> Mais tout n'est pas détruit, et vous en laissez vivre
> Un ... (ll. 1445-46)

Her recovery only manages to confuse Thésée all the more.

Indeed the possibility of self-betrayal is a constant preoccupation of the characters and reinforces the requirement of vigilance over their language, whether this is successful or not. Junie tells Britannicus:

> Combien de fois, hélas! puisqu'il faut vous le dire,
> Mon cœur de son désordre allait-il vous instruire?
> (ll. 999-1000)

Bajazet uses the word 'efforts' (l. 999) in terms of concealing his secret, having a moment previously explained the nature of those efforts:

> Croyez qu'il m'a fallu, dans ce moment cruel,
> Pour garder jusqu'au bout un silence perfide
> Rappeler tout l'amour que j'ai pour Atalide.
> (ll. 996-98)

Bajazet admits to Roxane herself that on several occasions he has even wanted to tell her of the secret he has concealed (ll. 1491-92). But Atalide too has been subject to the pressures of self-betrayal, as she explains to Bajazet:

> O ciel! combien de fois je l'aurais éclaircie,
> Si je n'eusse à sa haine exposé que ma vie. (ll. 749-50)

The consequences of self-betrayal are of course enormous, as Monime discovers when she falls for the trap Mithridate sets her. But in no play are they more costly than in *Phèdre* where self-betrayal is also a function of the momentum of language I have examined earlier. Phèdre breaks down a little more as each speech progresses during her first meeting with Hippolyte, until she realises too late that she has said more than she had intended:

> je m'égare,
> Seigneur; ma folle ardeur malgré moi se déclare. (ll. 629-30)

The consequences of self-betrayal are brought home to Phèdre later in the play when she is on the point of interceding on behalf of Hippolyte but is informed instead of his love for Aricie:

> Qui sait même où m'allait porter ce repentir?
> Peut-être à m'accuser j'aurais pu consentir;
> Peut-être, si la voix ne m'eût été coupée,
> L'affreuse vérité me serait échappée. (ll. 1199-1202)

Monime realises all too well that there are no half measures in revelation. Even the slightest sign is significant. Xipharès does not know of her love:

> Les dieux m'ont secouru, et mon cœur affermi
> N'a rien dit, ou du moins n'a parlé qu'à demi. (ll. 409-10)

Such a revelation would not have been harmful in the case of the prince, although her own declaration is the beginning of their troubles, but it illustrates the illusions characters entertain about the consequences of speech. On the other hand, a character (in this case Hermione) may not be aware of what is revealed by seemingly the most innocent of remarks. Oreste knows exactly the place he has in the heart of Hermione when she remarks: 'Vous que j'ai plaint enfin, que je voudrais aimer' (l. 535).

The characters' manifest lack of faith in their own capacities of performance is central to the idea of self-betrayal.[13] They are concerned by the possible transparency of their speech. With Atalide it is Bajazet's weakness which concerns her: 'Car enfin Bajazet ne sait point se cacher' (l. 391). Pyrrhus himself admits in his only meeting with Hermione an inability to act hypocritically: 'Et je soutiendrais mal ce que je ne crois pas' (l. 1280). Some characters are aware of the conditions where such transparency can become apparent and are prepared to exploit that awareness. Roxane knows that love may lead to unintended revelations:

> Ils ont beau se cacher, l'amour le plus discret
> Laisse par quelque marque échapper son secret.
> Observons Bajazet; étonnons Atalide. (ll. 1119-21)

Mithridate follows the same train of thought:

> L'amour avidement croit tout ce qui le flatte.
> Qui peut de son vainqueur mieux parler que l'ingrate?
> (ll. 1027-28)

Clytemnestre aims to test Agamemnon's powers of performance to the full: 'Voyons s'il soutiendra son indigne artifice' (l. 1150). Her questions then set him a number of linguistic traps. We already know of the king's weakness in betraying his grief (see ll. 209-12). Pharnace warns against the deceitful ways of the king which can lay the sort of trap set by Roxane and Clytemnestre:

> Sa haine sait cacher ses trompeuses adresses.
> Allons. Puisqu'il le faut, je marche sur vos pas;
> Mais en obéissant, ne nous trahissons pas. (ll. 372-74)

It is not surprising then that, the possibilities of self-betrayal being what they are, characters should prefer absence to the demands of presence. As Bajazet advises Atalide:

> Daignez de la sultane éviter la présence:
> Vos pleurs vous trahiraient; cachez-les à ses yeux. (ll. 673-74)

Atalide emphasises rather that their mutual presence before Roxane would betray them both:

> Allez. Entre elle et vous je ne dois point paraître;
> Votre trouble ou le mien nous ferait reconnaître. (ll. 789-90)

The words 'présence' and 'trouble' appear in *Athalie* as two elements leading to the revelation of a secret. Josabet is concerned at her appearance in the same place with Eliacin:

> Autant que je le puis j'évite sa présence,
> De peur qu'en le voyant quelque trouble indiscret
> Ne fasse avec mes pleurs échapper mon secret. (ll. 192-94)

Joad later suspects his wife of unwittingly disclosing the identity of the boy:

> Au perfide Mathan qui l'aurait révélé?
> Votre trouble à Mathan n'a-t-il point trop parlé? (ll. 1049-50)

'Trouble' also features in the reason for Monime's refusal to greet Mithridate on the shore: 'Je ne paraîtrai pas dans le trouble où je suis' (l. 422). She is obviously concerned at this stage that she might reveal her feelings for Xipharès. After Aricie has interrupted herself in time in order not to divulge the truth about Phèdre, she prefers flight:

> J'imite sa pudeur, et fuis votre présence
> Pour n'être pas forcée à rompre le silence. (ll. 1449-50)

It seems that absence is the only way to prevent speech at all. Monime bans Xipharès from her sight in order to avoid their love from becoming apparent:

> Dans ce dessein vous-même, il faut me soutenir,
> Et de mon faible cœur m'aider à vous bannir.
> J'attends du moins, j'attends de votre complaisance
> Que désormais partout vous fuirez ma présence. (ll. 701-4)

His presence would only provoke 'quelque indigne soupir' (l. 730). But absence in Racine is an illusion. It never works. The effacement of Atalide is precisely what leads to the death of Bajazet in the end. Thésée eventually learns the truth from Phèdre who is forced to make one last appearance on the stage after her attempts at effacement.

Absence of course implies silence and silence is an important part of speech in Racine, since it too is problematic in placing the characters under a good deal of pressure. Silences can occur within dialogue and they are always wounding because they reveal something unwelcome. In the meeting between Hermione and Pyrrhus in Act IV of *Andromaque* Pyrrhus obviously fails to respond to Hermione's plea to defer the wedding and merits the response: 'Vous ne répondez point? Perfide, je le voi' (l. 1375). Britannicus, misunderstanding the silence of Junie, becomes exasperated:

> Songiez-vous aux douleurs que vous m'alliez coûter?
> Vous ne me dites rien? (ll. 706-7)

In *Bérénice* silence is accompanied by bodily gesture:

> Eh bien, Seigneur? Mais quoi? sans me répondre
> Vous détournez les yeux, et semblez vous confondre?
> (ll. 595-96)

Mithridate is well aware of the significance of Monime's silence:

> Vous demeurez muette, et loin de me parler,
> Je vois, malgré vos soins, vos pleurs prêts à couler.
> (ll. 581-82)

The revelations of silence can also be represented in the line distribution in certain parts of the plays. In Act II, scene 4 of *Mithridate* Monime speaks for 7 lines out of 77. In the scene referred to earlier in *Britannicus* Junie's speeches occupy 9 out of 51 lines.

One thing is certain. Silence is an aspect of suffering. Xipharès complains that in the past: 'Tout mon amour alors ne put pas éclater' (l. 198). The suffering silence incurs is most acute with Phèdre who is 'atteinte d'un mal qu'elle s'obstine à taire' (l. 45). Silence in her case is perceived as the prelude to death: 'Elle meurt dans mes bras d'un mal qu'elle me cache' (l. 146). The frustration of silence is described by Acomat to Osmin as: 'L'embarras irritant de ne s'oser parler' (l. 160).

But, crucially, silence in Racine is difficult, and more often than not, impossible to maintain. Axiane, looking back on her relationship with Porus, laments:

> Et pourquoi te cachais-je avec tant de détours
> Un secret si fatal au repos de tes jours?
> Combien de fois, tes yeux forçant ma résistance,
> Mon cœur s'est-il vu près de rompre le silence? (ll. 977-80)

Monime too is aware of the difficulty silence presents:

> Hélas! si tu savais, pour garder le silence,
> Combien ce triste cœur s'est fait de violence. (ll. 411-12)

It is interesting that 'violence' rhymes with 'silence' on at least ten occasions in the plays and four of those examples occur in *Phèdre*.[14]

As some of the above quotations imply, the breaking of silence represents an end to constraint. At the beginning of the action of *Mithridate* Xipharès can no longer contain his love for Monime: 'Je l'aime, et ne veux plus m'en taire' (l. 35). She can no longer conceal hers: 'Oui, Prince, il n'est plus temps de le dissimuler' (l. 674). Hippolyte breaks his silence to Aricie and reveals a secret 'que mon cœur ne peut plus renfermer' (ll. 526-28). Later Phèdre is forced to admit: 'il faut rompre un injuste silence' (l. 1617).

Antiochus has suffered in silence for five years: 'Quoi qu'il en soit, parlons: c'est assez nous contraindre' (l. 48).

But, as with physical absence, there is an illusion attached to silence. Once characters have broken it, they believe that they can return to it. Pharnace urges Xipharès not to fall into the trap that Mithridate might set (ll. 367-74). Monime too thinks that she can retreat into silence after declaring her love for Xipharès:

> Je vous le dis, Seigneur, pour ne plus vous le dire,
> Ma gloire me rappelle et m'entraîne à l'autel,
> Où je vais vous jurer un silence éternel. (ll. 696-98)

Antiochus's declaration will, he hopes, be followed by another eternal silence:

> Je me suis tu cinq ans,
> Madame, et vais encor me taire plus longtemps. (ll. 209-10)

He is at that moment unaware that Titus will ask him to act as his messenger.

A return to silence is a major component of the structure of *Phèdre*. Œnone, right at the beginning of the play, almost as a presage of the outcome of a more important silence, urges Phèdre to erase the memory of her mother's misfortunes from her mind:

> Oublions-les, Madame, et qu'à tout l'avenir
> Un silence éternel cache ce souvenir. (ll. 251-52)

Hippolyte can barely relate to Théramène the horror of Phèdre's confession:

> Phèdre ... Mais non, grands dieux! qu'en un profond oubli
> Cet horrible secret demeure enseveli. (ll. 719-20)

Œnone's success in persuading Thésée of Hippolyte's guilt depends on the cancellation of Phèdre's speech: 'Mon zèle n'a besoin que de votre silence' (l. 894). It is interesting that Phèdre expresses her desire to return to silence in terms of absence, the point at which we started. Phèdre exclaims: 'Cache-moi bien plutôt; je n'ai que trop parlé' (l. 740). Hippolyte urges a return to silence in asking that Aricie forget that he has ever spoken to her about what has occurred: 'Oubliez, s'il se peut, que je vous ai parlé' (l. 1348).

One thing is sure in Racinian tragedy. Words once spoken can never be erased. Once the frontier between speech and silence has been crossed there is no going back. Speech is forever on record. *Phèdre* incorporates two stages of silence, the initial revelations of all the characters which must then be suppressed on Thésée's return, and the re-emergence of speech from the attempts at this return to silence. The irrevocability of speech is underlined on a number of other occasions. Thésée cannot revoke the curse once it has been enunciated. He prays to Neptune: 'Ne précipite point tes funestes bienfaits' (ll. 1483). Agamemnon is unsuccessful in his attempts to revoke the order to sacrifice his daughter, and Hermione's order to Oreste cannot be rescinded. There are even dangers in returning to the previous state of non-speech, as Bajazet knows to be the case with Roxane:

> [...] après avoir osé me voir et me parler,
> Il était dangereux pour vous de reculer. (ll. 1512-13)

There is one more aspect of silence I would like to consider and that is where one form of language excludes another. We know what the specific issues are in a Racinian tragedy and we know too what the characters expect others to say. The form of silence I am alluding to involves a concept I should like to call silent language. In the beginning of *Andromaque* we learn of the various relationships which will be crucial to the outcome of the tragedy. Thus when Oreste and Pyrrhus meet for the first time they speak to each other in a very formal language which entirely conceals the underlying personal issues. On Oreste's part this redundancy of language is a deliberate strategy, since he has been advised by Pylade: 'Pressez, demandez tout, pour ne rien obtenir' (l. 140). We know too that Arbate's replies to Mithridate from lines 482sq are less than the full truth of the situation. More crucially, in the beginning of Act II, scene 2 of *Phèdre,* it is clear to the spectator that Hippolyte's formal language conceals the expression of his love, which Théramène has provoked in the previous act. In a more deliberate way, Agamemnon fails to divulge on a number of occasions the real reason for bringing Iphigénie to Aulis. Silent language is all the more significant when one character expects a very specific thing to be said. In this sense the whole of *Bajazet* could be said to rest on the concept of silent language. Roxane enquires of Atalide:

> Pourquoi faut-il au moins que, pour me consoler,
> L'ingrat ne parle pas comme on le fait parler? (ll. 275-76)

Bajazet maintains this 'silence' from the first to the third act but is forced out of it when confronted with the letter in Act V. In *Bajazet* it is almost as if Bajazet himself wishes to be elsewhere than in the stage space, especially since he has emerged reluctantly from a place of non-speech. By his refusal to say what is required he absents himself.

A very important example of silent language is Junie's attempt to dismiss Britannicus on the orders of Néron. She is obviously speaking a language which is not her own. Indeed the problem with this sort of silence is that it sometimes speaks.[15] Néron realises that he has failed in his attempts to rid himself of his rival since Junie's love has spoken even in her silence. Pharnace too believes that he has penetrated Monime's secret even though she has yet to declare herself to Xipharès: 'Je crois voir l'intérêt que vous voulez celer' (l. 289).

A number of comments are called for on the subject of silence in Racinian theatre. First, the absence of voice is often perceived by the characters as a deprivation, something confirmed by the very urgency with which Bérénice wishes to speak to Titus:

> Aussitôt, sans l'attendre, et sans être attendue,
> Je reviens le chercher, et dans cette entrevue
> Dire tout ce qu'aux cœurs l'un de l'autre contents
> Inspirent des transports retenus si longtemps. (ll. 323-36)

Later she reproaches Titus for his silence:

> J'entends que vous m'offrez un nouveau diadème,
> Et ne puis cependant vous entendre vous-même. (ll. 567-68)

Ismène observes that Hippolyte is deprived of a voice, even though he is in love: 'Mais il en a les yeux, s'il n'en a le langage' (l. 414). The possession of a voice is thus regarded as a special quality, the deprivation of which is a significant event. Phèdre describes her reaction on seeing Hippolyte for the first time: 'Je demeurai sans voix' (l. 65). The deprivation of voice is all the more terrible for being final. Junie expresses her anxiety at the forthcoming reconciliation of Britannicus with the emperor: 'Et si je vous parlais pour la dernière fois' (l. 1536). Bajazet is actively deprived of a voice at the effacement of Atalide in his encounters with Roxane. He does not know what to say: 'Eh bien! mais quels discours faut-il que je lui tienne?' (l. 786) Hippolyte comes to regard the power of speech as a dubious privilege to the extent that he would even like to be deprived of it. Rather than recount the horror of what he has heard: 'Qu'ils m'ôtent la parole et m'étouffent la voix' (l. 1080).

The second point about silence is that it is always something which must be explained.[16] Bérénice is adamant on this point: 'Et que dit ce silence?' (l. 627). Or again: 'Ah! qu'il m'explique un silence si rude' (l. 643). But that completeness is never less than tragic. Knowledge is a part of suffering. Racinian characters can take refuge neither in silence nor in speech. As Jacques Scherer comments: 'Dans l'univers de la parole coupable on ne doit ni parler ni se taire' (*Racine*, p.75).

Thirdly, silence exposes a character in a way that speech does not. Speech at least affords the possibility of concealment whereas silence reveals the fact of concealment — or refusal — itself. In an experience where the expectations of speech are so specific, the complete absence of speech is more critical than any attempt at evasion. Speech allows the character to prolong his or her existence, and maintains the expectation of the character addressed. Silence totally denies the validity of that expectation for the latter and may deny life to the former.

One of the major themes of this chapter has been the ways in which speaking rests on and generates what I have called the tension of utterance. I should now like to turn to the listener, perhaps a neglected aspect of Racinian language.[17] Certainly the structure of the plays as largely a succession of tirades means that Racinian characters do a lot of listening. Moreover, they also talk about the way they themselves listen and the ways they are listened to. Listening itself thus involves a tension. But it is also an activity in its own right, and, paraphrasing Barthes, one might say: 'Entendre, c'est faire' (p.66). In the specific context of Racine listening is crucial because the characters expect each other to say precise things. Hearing in this sense is as much an event as speaking.[18]

The importance of listening can be glimpsed from some examples of line distribution in particular scenes. In Act IV, scene 2 of *Britannicus* Néron speaks for 46 out of 190 lines and we know that it is for the actor a notoriously difficult scene to perform. Néron plays a listening role in other scenes: in Act IV, scene 3, with Burrhus, he has only 19.1/2 lines out of 107.1/2, and in scene 4 of the same act, this time with Narcisse, 22 out of 90 lines. In the whole of the fourth act, Néron speaks for 87 lines out of 365 lines. Line distribution in *Bérénice* is particularly telling where the focus is sometimes on Titus as a listener. In his first meeting with the queen he has only 13 in a scene of 68 lines. It is also interesting, however, to note how, on occasions, a transition takes place between speaking and listening. In Act I, scene 4 Bérénice dominates structurally the beginning of the scene, speaking for all but 3 of the 43 lines. She is then reduced to a listening role, Antiochus this time dominating by 89 out of 107. In Act V the position of Bérénice in the distribution is pivotal. She moves from a situation of listening to one of speaking, where indeed the responsibility for the conclusion of the action falls to her. From the beginning of Act V Thésée can only listen as the full truth of the situation is revealed to him. In fact, he can be held to be the target of speech from the point of his return, something equally true of Mithridate.

One cannot however conclude necessarily that speaking is equivalent to activity whereas listening signifies passivity.[19] Certainly speech is an imposition on others in the sense that there are victims of speech, among whom Junie is perhaps the best example. But, as I have noted, listening too is an imposition and an unwelcome one at that. Bajazet illustrates this perfectly. In the scene I have referred to between Antiochus and Bérénice, the 'silence' of the queen cannot be interpreted as passivity, nor the speech of Antiochus as an aspect of power. Bérénice's silence and the way she listens in fact confirm her position of power even in the eyes of Antiochus. The power relations of speech in Racinian tragedy are not limited to speaking.

How then do characters negotiate the act of listening? First, it is obvious that certain characters listen for specific signs in the speech of others which would satisfy their expectations. On many occasions those expectations are cruelly denied. Roxane wants to confirm that Bajazet loves her, as she has been led to believe. Yet her meetings with him fail to match her requirements:

> Je ne trouvais point ce trouble, cette ardeur
> Que m'avait tant promis un discours trop flatteur. (ll. 283-84)

Thésée orders Hippolyte in a series of questions to recount what has occurred. Hippolyte refuses to answer (ll. 979-83). In Act I, scene 3 of *Mithridate* Pharnace expects to hear Monime accept him as the rightful successor to his father only to be told of his unacceptability. The play in which denial of expectation is perhaps at its most intense is *Bérénice*. Phénice warns her mistress that: 'Titus n'a point encore expliqué sa pensée' (l. 292). After meeting with Titus for the first time since his emergence from his period of mourning, she exclaims: 'Quoi! me quitter sitôt, et ne me rien dire?' (l. 625)

Characters most often hear what they do not wish to hear. This does not prevent them from being prone to a compulsion to hear, in the same way that they suffer from a compulsion to speak. Characters require evidence and are not usually content to rely on the reports of others. Hermione reacts immediately to Oreste's observation that 'enfin il vous hait' (l. 549):

> Qui vous l'a dit, Seigneur, qu'il me méprise?
> Ses regards, ses discours, vous l'ont-ils donc appris? (l. 550-1)

Céphise believes that Andromaque should be satisfied with Pyrrhus' promise because she has just heard it in person (l. 1053). Roxane cannot remain satisfied with what she has been told: 'Ces gages incertains ne me peuvent suffire' (l. 286). Consequently: 'Moi-même j'ai voulu m'assurer de sa foi' (l. 279). The compulsion to hear is naturally connected to the demands of presence. Mithridate sends for Monime so that she should confirm in person her love for Xipharès:

> Qu'on appelle la reine. Oui, sans aller plus loin,
> Je veux l'ouïr. (ll. 1025-26)

Mithridate's eagerness to know is represented on another occasion by a flurry of questions:

> Qu'est-ce qui s'est passé? Qu'as-tu vu? Que sais-tu?
> Depuis quel temps, pourquoi, comment t'es-tu rendu?
> (ll. 481-82)

Characters of course must suffer unwelcome news. Antiochus must hear of the preparations for the marriage of Titus and Bérénice. Hermione is forced to listen to Cléone's account of the nuptials and then Oreste's account of the assassination. In the past Phèdre has ordered that Hippolyte's name should never be pronounced in her presence (ll. 603-4).

Urgency is a component of the desire to hear. Bérénice becomes increasingly frustrated with Antiochus' reluctance to deliver Titus's message: 'Je veux que vous parliez' (l. 883). Xipharès is desperate to know whether Monime loves him: 'On vient, Madame, on vient: expliquez-vous de grâce' (l. 219). The imperative to speak is a desire to hear, which is a desire to know. Œnone cannot wait a moment longer before Phèdre enunciates her terrible secret: 'Délivrez mon esprit de ce funeste doute' (l. 245). In *Phèdre* the desire to know is conditioned by the nature of what will be said. Thésée cannot possibly suspect the truth when he commands: 'Que Phèdre explique enfin le trouble où je la vois' (l. 987). The requirement of presence can also be used as a weapon. Néron forces unwelcome news on Britannicus:

> il vaut mieux que lui-même
> Entende son arrêt de la bouche qu'il aime. (ll. 667–68)

At times characters are unable to believe what they have heard and require the ears of others for confirmation. Bérénice is incredulous at Titus's failure to speak at their first meeting in the play and appeals to Phénice for assistance:

> Mais tu nous entendais. Il ne faut rien me taire:
> Parle. N'ai-je rien dit qui lui puisse déplaire? (ll. 635–36)

Acomat is sufficiently politically astute to issue the following order to Osmin:

> Demeure, et s'il le faut, sois prêt à confirmer
> Le récit important dont je vais l'informer. (ll. 211–12)

Emphasising how the momentous nature of what is said is important in the act of listening, Agamemnon describes his reaction at the pronouncement of Calchas on the oracle:

> Je sentis dans mon corps tout mon sang se glacer.
> Je demeurai sans voix. (ll. 64–5)

He also knows that the truth, when revealed to Clytemnestre, will be more than he can bear, which is why he wishes to avoid her presence (ll. 147–48). Phèdre reacts with horror at the very name of Hippolyte: 'Malheureuse, quel nom est sorti de ta bouche?' (ll. 206) Antiochus is aware of the nature of what he reveals to Bérénice on two occasions in the play. In this way Bérénice is always a reluctant listener. Her language indicates what she thinks of his first declaration:

> J'oublie en sa faveur un discours qui m'outrage.
> Je n'en ai point troublé le cours injurieux. (ll. 264–65)

The momentous nature of what is to be said can also induce a reluctance to hear in the listener which complements the compulsion to know that I have commented on earlier. The moment may not be right and speech may be inopportune. Titus at last comes to tell Bérénice that they must separate, to which she responds: 'Ah! cruel! est-il temps de me le déclarer?' (l. 1062) This is not, in other words, the moment at which I wish to hear this. Mithridate similarly hears too late that Monime refuses to marry him (ll. 1302–3). Thésée wants to avoid hearing Hippolyte's defence of his love for Aricie: 'Cesse, cesse, et m'épargne un importun discours' (l. 1135).

Characters are sometimes aware of the need to spare others the full horror of the truth and Hippolyte's reluctance to speak derives from the nature of what he would have to say:

> Ai-je dû mettre au jour l'opprobre de son lit?
> Devais-je, en lui faisant un récit trop sincère,
> D'une indigne rougeur couvrir le front d'un père?
> (ll. 1340–42)

Phèdre of course fails to spare Œnone, and later Hippolyte, but is aware that she should have done:

> Mes fureurs au dehors ont osé se répandre:
> J'ai dit ce que jamais on ne devait entendre. (ll. 741–42)[20]

The reaction of the characters to the horror of what they hear is clearly marked by Racine in the varied responses it produces. Bajazet is aghast at the idea that a marriage with Roxane should take place before the end of the day: 'Ah! que proposez-vous, Madame?' (l. 451) Achille cannot contain himself at the new of the sacrifice: 'Ce discours sans horreur se peut-il écouter?' (l. 915) Bérénice's response to Antiochus's declaration of love is expressed as: 'Ah! que me dites-vous?' (l. 209) Likewise Monime exclaims: 'Ah! que m'apprenez-vous?' (l. 191) Or, when Xipharès fears she may be in love with Pharnace: 'Ah! qu'entends-je moi-même?' (l. 640) Emphasis on hearing is indeed common among the characters. Roxane reproaches Bajazet with her question: 'Quoi donc? Que dites-vous? Et que viens-je d'entendre?' (l. 561) Hippolyte cannot believe what Phèdre has just told him: 'Dieux! qu'est-ce que j'entends' (l. 663).

These reactions are of course conventional in seventeenth-century drama. But Racine's emphasis on the whole thematics of speaking and listening surely adds another dimension to them. Within the context of listening the word 'oreille' is less frequent than 'bouche' and, in the instances in which it occurs less significant. One example of its use, however, embodies the comments I have just made and that is Phèdre's reaction on hearing the news that Hippolyte loves Aricie: 'Quelle nouvelle a frappé mon oreille?' *Phèdre*, as I have had occasion to note, is a play above all of pronouncement, of coming to say what should never have been said, of hearing what should never have been heard. The whole structure of the play represents the transition from silence to language.

So far I have considered the position of the listener reacting to what is said. Of course characters also become speakers and it seems natural that the speaker should envisage the position of the listener in what he or she is about to say. Listening itself, if its nature is to be understood, has to be spoken. This may take the form of knowing in advance how the addressee will respond. Oreste hears in his mind his eventual dismissal by Hermione:

> Déjà même je crois entendre la réponse
> Qu'en secret contre moi votre haine prononce. (ll. 517–18)

Antiochus is full of foreboding at the manner in which Bérénice will receive him at their first meeting in the play:

> Dois-je croire qu'au rang où Titus la destine
> Elle m'écoute mieux que dans la Palestine? (ll. 27–28)

He also imagines her position as listener at the moment he delivers Titus's message that she must leave:

> L'aimable Bérénice entendrait de ma bouche
> Qu'on l'abandonne? Ah, Reine! et qui l'aurait pensé
> Que ce mot dût jamais vous être prononcé? (ll. 836–38)

Œnone appeals to the fact that she will not be as useful in Phèdre's defence as Phèdre herself: she will not be heard as she should:

> Vous-même en expirant appuyez ses discours.
> A votre accusateur que pourrai-je répondre? (ll. 875–76)

Earlier, however, Phèdre argues that Œnone will be much more effective as a plaintiff than her and that Hippolyte will hear her better: 'Tes discours trouveront plus d'accès que les miens' (l. 808).

That the characters sometimes project themselves as listeners is confirmed by the way in which they often prepare their interlocutors for the contents of their impending speech. Before relaying to Titus the opinions of the Romans on his projected marriage, Paulin warns him: 'Vous m'avez commandé surtout d'être sincère' (l. 403). Antiochus too tries to indicate to Bérénice the serious import of the message he is about to impart:

> Mais ne vous flattez point: je vais vous annoncer
> Peut-être des malheurs où vous n'osez penser. (ll. 889–90)

Xipharès signals to Arbate the significance of the fact that he loves the woman who is betrothed to his father: 'Je m'en vais t'étonner' (l. 32). On two occasions Phèdre prepares Œnone — and perhaps herself — for the news of her love for Hippolyte: 'Tu frémiras d'horreur si je romps le silence' (l. 238). Or again: 'Tu vas ouïr le comble des horreurs' (l. 260).

Equally, Acomat makes quite certain that Roxane is ready to receive what he has to say to her: 'Et la sultane est-elle en état de m'entendre?' (l. 1375) Indeed it could be argued that Roxane's character explores in some fundamental ways states of listening, especially when she seems to hear, in the off-stage scene of reconciliation between her and Bajazet, positive signs of encouragement he has failed to enunciate. Roxane is in effect an example of where the preparation of the listener has been only too effective. Roxane's receptivity has been manipulated by Acomat in persuading her of Bajazet's charms. As a result of his rhetoric:

> La sultane éperdue
> N'eut plus d'autre désir que celui de sa vue. (ll. 141–41)

The very atmosphere can add to the intensity of the process of listening. Acomat refers to a moment:

> Où Roxane attentive écoutait son amant.
> Tout gardait devant eux un auguste silence. (ll. 880–1)

In *Britannicus* Narcisse is urged by Britannicus: 'Examine leurs yeux, observe leurs discours' (l. 349). I have referred to these lines in the context of the visual and the vocal as an imperative in the plays of Racine. It could equally well serve as the paradigm for the situation of listening. Characters are always listening for verbal signs which may sometimes be accompanied by bodily gesture. In any case, as I have observed, listening is an activity in which the whole being of the character is engaged. Listening is not leisure and the imperative to listen only serves to confirm this. Oreste wants Hermione to listen carefully: 'Eh bien, Madame, eh bien! écoutez donc Oreste' (l. 409). No doubt exists as to the attitude Roxane expects from Bajazet: 'Bajazet, écoutez' (l. 538).

That speakers are very attentive to the reactions of their interlocutors is marked in the way they often notice surprise. Xipharès comments to Arbate after revealing his love for Monime: 'Tu ne t'attendais pas, sans doute, à ce discours' (l. 37) Surprise obviously appears on Monime's face when he confronts her with his love:

> Mais avec quelque ennui que vous puissiez apprendre
> Cet amour criminel qui vient de vous surprendre. (ll. 175–76)

Mithridate's plan to march on Rome surprises everybody. As he notes: 'Ce dessein vous surprend' (l. 787). Pharnace admits that he has been unable to conceal his own surprise (l. 863). Hippolyte indicates that surprise is not a weak reaction when he says to Théramène after hearing Phèdre's declaration of love: 'Théramène, fuyons, ma surprise est extrême' (l. 717).

One element in speech which comes under particular scrutiny by the listener is the tone of the speaker. Bérénice complains to Titus:

> Hé quoi? vous me jurez une éternelle ardeur,
> Et vous me la jurez avec cette froideur? (ll. 589–90)

Roxane too refers to the 'discours glacé' of Bajazet (l. 1035) and Hippolyte is disturbed at Aricie's reaction to his proposal that she accompany him in his flight from Trézène: 'Quand je suis tout de feu, d'où vous vient cette glace?' (l. 1374) On other occasions characters observe grief on the part of those they address and this may be in the form of sound. Monime tells Xipharès that she cannot belong to him: 'J'entends, vous gémissez' (l. 699).[21] Roxane reproaches Bajazet: 'Tu soupires enfin, et sembles te troubler' (559). Facial expression in the listener is clearly apparent. Monime says to Mithridate: 'Seigneur, vous changez de visage!' (l. 1112) Other bodily gestures are perceived.[22] Britannicus cannot understand the reaction of Junie just before he sees Néron for the meeting of reconciliation:

> D'où vient qu'en m'écoutant, vos yeux, vos tristes yeux
> Avec de longs regards se tournent vers les cieux? (ll. 1489–90)

Assuérus observes a similar gesture with Esther: 'Je vois qu'en m'écoutant vos yeux s'adressent au ciel' (l. 682). It may be that the contents of speech are expected to produce a particular physical reaction in the listener. Hippolyte remarks to Aricie:

> Peut-être le récit d'un amour si sauvage
> Vous fait en m'écoutant rougir de votre ouvrage. (ll. 553–54)

Or a reaction is not forthcoming at all. Bajazet fails to move Atalide:

> Je vois enfin, je vois qu'en ce même moment
> Tout ce que je vous dis vous touche faiblement. (ll. 1003–4)

Indeed characters often comment on how others seem not to have been listening to them at all. They may be mistaken in that assumption, as Phèdre is with Hippolyte:

> Ciel! comme il m'écoutait! Par combien de détours
> L'insensible a longtemps éludé mes discours! (ll. 743–44)

She later fears appearing before Hippolyte: 'Le cœur gros de soupirs qu'il n'a point écoutés' (l. 840). Œnone however complains that she is not listened to by Phèdre who is 'sourde à tous nos discours' (l. 187). Axiane too complains that her words of love cannot heard by Porus:

Mais que sert de pousser des soupirs superflus
Qui se perdent en l'air et que tu n'entends plus. (ll. 991–92)

Characters are aware that not being listened to constitutes a form of rejection. Jocaste finds herself in this position with Polynice:

Mais il ne m'entend plus:
Aussi bien que mes pleurs mes cris sont superflus. (ll. 573–74)

Later they both reject her in the same way (ll. 1029–30). Xipharès experiences the same emotion with Monime: 'Elle me fuit, et ne veut plus m'entendre' (l. 747) This however represents Monime's realisation that what she has heard is dangerous enough. Junie too has already heard too much from Néron and is distraught at her enforced farewell to Britannicus. Néron tries to detain her: 'Non, Seigneur, je ne puis rien entendre' (l. 744). A refusal to listen can therefore be willful. Phèdre reaches a stage where the advice of Œnone is no longer welcome: 'Je ne t'écoute plus' (l. 1317). The failure to listen is clearly an act as well as the display of an attitude, since it can mark a change in relationship and a transformation in the relations of power. Junie's refusal to listen is a direct indication of her refusal to be an accomplice of Néron in his battle for power with his mother. Listening would constitute betrayal.

Indeed the silence I have explored earlier also constitutes a reaction to speech. It is a function of listening and can represent the degree to which listening is an imposition. Agamemnon can only stand and listen to Achille who is expecting the arrival of Iphigénie in Aulis. Achille of course has returned too soon. Because Agamemnon cannot speak the truth without displaying his emotion he must suffer others speaking for him, with the full knowledge of the implications of what they say. After the first scene of Act I Agamemnon speaks for 71 of 234 lines despite being on stage the whole time. The news of Thésée's death renders Phèdre speechless and Œnone speaks for Phèdre. It is as if Panope is awaiting a reply from Phèdre but it is Œnone who takes it upon herself to confirm that Phèdre is still listening:

La reine qui t'entend
Ne négligera point cet avis important. (ll. 335–56)

Monime and Xipharès have to suffer in silence as Mithridate recounts the treachery of his son, whom Mithridate believes to be and whom Xipharès takes to be Pharnace. One can only reconstruct what Monime is meant to think as she listens. What too should be the reaction of Xipharès as he listens for quite a proportion of Act I, scene 3 to Pharnace and Monime? The situation is reversed in the latter part of the scene when Monime listens to the argument between the two brothers. The only information that we have with which to interpret this listening situation is that both brothers love Monime. It is surely important too that Œnone hears every word that Phèdre says to Hippolyte in Act II, scene 5. The silent listener is often a feature of Racinian tragedy and reminds us that Racinan dialogue does not take place in the 'huis-clos' that is so often held to characterise the plays.[23]

There are times however in the plays when characters entertain illusions about the way in which they have been heard or may be heard. Oreste fools himself into thinking that he has been on the verge of a breakthrough with Hermione: 'Ses yeux s'ouvraient, Pylade, elle écoutait Oreste' (l. 745). Titus's unwitting misjudgement of the relationship which now obtains between Bérénice and Antiochus could not be more ironical. He attempts to persuade Antiochus to be his messenger with the words: 'Elle ne voit dans Rome et n'écoute que vous' (l. 697). Not only does Antiochus delude himself about the reception of his declaration: 'Au lieu de s'offenser, elle pourrait me plaindre' (l. 47). But he even manages to misjudge the reaction of Bérénice in the beginning of the play. He tells her:

> Je vois que votre cœur m'applaudit en secret,
> Je vois que l'on m'écoute avec moins de regret,
> Et que trop attentive à ce récit funeste,
> En faveur de Titus vous pardonnez le reste. (ll. 225–28)

What could lead him to misread the signs in this way?

Listening is on rare occasions pleasurable. Cléofile tells Ephestion, Alexandre's messenger: 'J'écoute avec plaisir le récit de sa flamme' (l. 394). Aricie cannot contain her excitement at the possibility that Hippolyte loves her:

> Que mon cœur, chère Ismène, écoute avidement
> Un discours qui peut-être a peu de fondement! (ll. 415–6)

Monime describes to Xipharès her feelings when listening to his declaration of love:

> Et lorsque ce matin j'en écoutais le cours,
> Mon cœur vous répondait tous vos mêmes discours. (ll. 689–90)

How much pleasure, however, should the actress reveal at the moment of the declaration itself?[24] Monime in fact informs Xipharès that he should have realised sooner that she loved him: 'Quel amour ai-je enfin sans colère écouté?' (l. 670) Confusion is sometimes pleasurable. Despite her desires, Aricie describes herself to Hippolyte as 'étonnée et confuse' (l. 509), whereas certainly Junie is incredulous and hurt at Néron's declaration: 'Seigneur, avec raison je demeure étonnée' (l. 603).

But apprehension and suffering are more common. This is manifest in the attention they pay to the difficulties they themselves experience in listening to others. Néron is concerned at the way in which he will be able to hear his mother list all the instances of his ingratitude: 'De quel front soutenir ce long entretien?' (l. 489) Antiochus again deludes himself that he may renew his relationship with Bérénice:

> J'ai vu tous mes projets tant de fois démentis,
> Que j'écoute en tremblant tout ce que tu me dis. (ll. 1281–82)

Iphigénie can wait no longer for Arcas to explain himself on the real situation in Aulis: 'Je tremble. Expliquez-vous, Arcas' (l. 907) Junie has suffered at the reaction of Britannicus in Act II, scene 6:

> Quel tourment de se taire en voyant ce qu'on aime,
> De l'entendre gémir, de l'affliger soi-même. (ll. 1003–4)

Bewilderment too can enter into the feelings of the character who listens. Thésée cannot penetrate fully the meaning of Aricie's refusal to divulge the real truth of the situation and can only ask:

> Quelle est donc sa pensée? et que cache un discours
> Commencé tant de fois, interrompu toujours? (ll. 1451–52)

Mithridate's bewilderment derives from his inability to speak while listening to the defiance of Monime:

> Elle me quitte! Et moi, dans un lâche silence,
> Je semble de sa fuite approuver l'insolence? (ll. 1379–80)

Most poignantly of all characters not only hear the voices of others: they hear their own. Hermione recognises the consequences of her order to kill Pyrrhus (she repeats 'à le vouloir' of line 1420): 'A le vouloir? Hé quoi? c'est donc moi qui l'ordonne?' (l. 1421).[25] Antiochus anticipates hearing himself give the message to Bérénice that she must leave Rome:

> Entrons chez Bérénice; et puisqu'on nous l'ordonne,
> Allons lui déclarer que Titus l'abandonne ...
> Mais plutôt demeurons. Que faisais-je? Est-ce à moi,
> Arsace, à me charger de ce cruel emploi? (ll. 831–34)

Bérénice, in Act IV, scene 5, cannot believe the words she has uttered:

> Je n'écoute plus rien, et pour jamais: adieu ...
> Pour jamais! Ah! Seigneur! (ll. 1110–11)

Phèdre is the character most acutely aware of the sound of her own voice. She is conscious of having barely disguised her desire to be watching Hippolyte at his favourite activity: 'Insensée, où suis-je? et qu'ai-je dit?' (l. 179) Later she urges Thésée to avenge her for her son's love for Aricie but realises the enormity of using the wronged husband to wreak revenge on behalf of the wrongdoer: 'Chaque mot sur mon front fait dresser mes cheveux' (l. 1268).[26] If only Néron too could have heard himself speak. Burrhus cannot believe that Néron has been able to utter his famous 'J'embrasse mon rival, mais c'est pour l'étouffer' (l. 1304) without a feeling of horror: 'Vous-même sans frémir avez-vous pu l'entendre?' (l. 1318).

Listening, then, is an integral part of the suffering the characters undergo in the course of the tragic experience, and replicates in many ways the tensions that are inherent in speaking. Moreover listening is not without its risks, since the pressures placed on communication in Racinian tragedy can lead characters to mishear, all of which is consequential in its own way. Certainly Pyrrhus misreads the tone of Hermione's first speech in Act IV, scene 5 since he interprets it as 'indifférence'. His error leads to one of the most scathing attacks launched on a character in the whole of Racinian tragedy. *Phèdre* is full of mishearing. In the first place, Œnone misjudges her mistress's horror at hearing the name of Hippolyte, thinking that she is merely angry at Hippolyte's succession to the throne of his father (l. 206 sq). Later Hippolyte 'mishears' Phèdre on three occasions: when she refers to her grief in lines 615–17 and when he naively speaks of her love for Thésée in lines 631–33. Finally his failure to understand the real import of her evocation of the episode of the slaying of the minotaur leads to Phèdre's outburst: 'Ah! cruel, tu m'as trop entendue!' Thésée in his turn fails to read correctly two silences. The first is Phèdre's: 'Le silence de Phèdre épargnait ce coupable!' (l. 1013). The second is that of Hippolyte himself in line 1023.

The word 'entendre', whose ambiguity underlines the relation of hearing to understanding or misunderstanding, is fully brought out on a number of occasions, as in the following accusation thrown at Monime: 'Je vous entends ici mieux que vous ne pensez' (l. 586). If characters believe that to hear is to understand then they must get it right first time.[27] In this case, of course, Mithridate gets it wrong. Usually no second chances are offered for correction. In any case it is clear enough that characters do not mean all they say or do not say all they mean. But the connection of hearing with understanding marks listening out even more as a crucial activity in the drama. Often the characters are all too correct in their interpretation of their interlocutors, Oreste in particular. He knows all too well the real place he occupies in the heart of Hermione:

> Je vous entends. Tel est mon partage funeste:
> Le cœur est pour Pyrrhus, et les vœux pour Oreste. (ll. 537–38)

Pharnace understands that Monime and Xipharès love each other:

> J'entends que votre cœur soupire;
> Et j'ai conçu l'adieu qu'elle vient de vous dire. (ll. 339–40)

If it is necessary to interpret correctly, then characters must believe what is said to them. Very often listening marks disbelief, which is in a sense a suspension of judgement, since it requires confirmation. Antiochus has difficulty in accepting the contents of the message he must convey to Bérénice: 'Dois-je croire, grands dieux! ce que je viens d'ouïr?' (l. 777) Nor can, initially, Oreste believe his luck in hearing Hermione address him as if she desired him: 'Mais, de grâce, est-ce à moi que ce discours s'adresse?' (l. 530) His disbelief resurfaces on a second occasion after she has denied the sincerity of her desire to kill Pyrrhus: 'Que vois-je? Est-ce Hermione? Et que viens-je d'entendre?' (l. 1565) The cruellest moment of disbelief is that of Bérénice when Antiochus finally delivers his message: 'Nous séparer? Qui? Moi? Titus de Bérénice?' (l. 895) Disbelief is often connected with words that should not have been expressed in the first place. Equally they should never have been heard. This means that, however sincere is the person who gives the news, he will inevitably be disbelieved, as Antiochus realises to his cost:

> Avec quelle injustice et quelle indignité
> Elle doute à mes yeux de ma sincérité! (ll. 933–34)

If this is the case there is no code whatsoever that can allow one character to distinguish the level of sincerity of another. It is something that concerns Junie in Néron. She asks Britannicus: 'Mais me répondez-vous de sa sincérité?' (l. 1496) The answer is easy for the spectator to provide since we know of Néron's real motives. It is less easy for one character to interpret the words of another. Listening is thus a continual process of assessment. Relaxation is impossible. Why should Monime not have believed Mithridate's desire that his favourite son should marry her instead of him? Perhaps she is naive in her interpretation of human behaviour, in spite of all she knows of the king's past:

> Mais enfin je vous crois, et je ne puis penser
> Qu'à feindre si longtemps vous puissiez vous forcer. (ll. 1097–98)

Credibility and listening are connected most strongly in *Bajazet*. After all Roxane has been led to believe in Bajazet's love by what Atalide has reported to her. She now wants to hear him herself. Atalide tries to divert her from this course of action: 'Et pourquoi de son cœur doutez-vous aujourd'hui?' (l. 267) But Roxane is concerned at having to believe a third party: 'Hélas! pour mon repos que ne le puis-je croire?' (l. 274) But there are signs that Roxane does not need to hear in order to believe. Bajazet, explaining his so-called reconciliation with Roxane, reports:

> A peine ai-je parlé que, sans presque m'entendre,
> Ses pleurs précipités ont coupé mes discours. (ll. 986–87)

Both Bajazet and Atalide refer to her 'crédulité' (l. 376 and l. 991). In this case it is suggested that listening is a matter of disposition. Atalide remarks: 'Mais qu'aisément l'amour croit tout ce qu'il souhaite' (l. 373). (Indeed Mithridate relies on just such a belief: 'L'amour avidement croit tout ce qui le flatte' (l. 1027).) Roxane is finally disabused (referring herself to 'crédulité' (l. 1297)) but significantly not by what she hears, although she entertains enough doubts on that score, but by the discovery of a letter from Bajazet concealed on the person of Atalide.

It is perhaps appropriate at this stage that I should deal with soliloquy which poses a number of problems in terms of the speaker and the addressee, and reemphasises a number of the above points.[28] The most common device in the soliloquies of Racine is the interrogative form where the characters ask themselves a certain number of questions, the answers to which may or may not be forthcoming. The soliloquy is thus a means by which a character can discuss future strategy or a particular moral problem.[29] In the stances of Antigone in Act V, scene 1 she attempts to decide whether she should imitate the example of her mother and commit suicide, or live. It is useful to note that her debate is straightforward without any intimation of what should be said in future or without any reflexion on what has been said in the past. Titus too, in Act IV, scene 4, addresses the problem of his future actions, but, as we shall see later, his soliloquy is also a direct reflexion on language and how he will pronounce his order that Bérénice should leave Rome.

Characters also address other characters in the course of their soliloquies. Axiane addresses Porus, lamenting that she did not reveal her love for him earlier, having preferred to hide behind considerations of her own reputation (l. 985). She then reconstructs what she ought to have told him (l. 986 sq). The soliloquy here represents a lost opportunity which, as she believes at this stage, will never return, and underlines the potential that exists at any stage of dialogue. Characters choose some words to the exclusion of others. In Act II, scene 3, Oreste addresses Hermione, but in a way which would not have been possible in the course of his previous scene with her. Whereas Axiane laments the absence of Porus, Oreste can only be triumphant and superior to Hermione in her absence. Oreste's triumph in this scene is of course short-lived.

Other soliloquies, however, provide opportunities whereby characters reflect on what has just been heard and the way in which it has been said. Phèdre, like Axiane, considers what might have taken place if she had been allowed to speak on Hippolyte's behalf before being cut short by the news of Hippolyte's love for Aricie (ll. 1199–1202). Soliloquies may on the other hand constitute more specifically critiques of the way others have spoken or listened. Hermione has been stunned by the reception of Pyrrhus in Act IV, scene 5: 'Le cruel! de quel œil il m'a congédiée' (l. 1397). She describes his failure to pity her or even to speak to her:

> L'ai-je vu se troubler et me plaindre un moment?
> En ai-je pu tirer un seul gémissement?
> Muet à mes soupirs, tranquille à mes alarmes,
> Semblait-il seulement qu'il eût part à mes larmes?
> (ll. 1399–1403)

Her speech is also then a critique of her failure to move him sufficiently. In a similar way, Mithridate comments on the way in which he has listened to the defiance of Monime:

> Elle me quitte! Et moi, dans un lâche silence,
> Je semble de sa fuite approuver l'insolence?
> (ll. 1379–80)

Oreste in his turn is incredulous at his dismissal by Hermione after his return from the wedding ceremony: 'Que vois-je? Est-ce Hermione? Et que viens-je d'entendre?' (l. 1565)

Reflexions on previous speech are common enough in other tragedies of Racine. This may be in the form of what has been discovered. Roxane knows in Act IV, scene 4 that Atalide loves Bajazet: 'Ma rivale à mes yeux s'est enfin déclarée' (l. 1209). As with Oreste a character may reflect on the credibility of a previous enunciation. This is the case with Mithridate:

> Je ne le croirai point? Vain espoir qui me flatte!
> Tu ne le crois que trop, malheureux Mithridate! (ll. 1007–8)

Or bewilderment may ensue. Roxane is unsure of what to believe after eliciting a hesitant and ambiguous response from Atalide: 'De tout ce que je vois que faut-il que je pense?' (l. 1065) In Act V, scene 4 Thésée too is bewildered by Aricie's silence.

Complementing reflexions on previous speech, the soliloquy sometimes performs the function of a consideration of what must be said. The soliloquy in this sense faces both ways. Antiochus, in Act I, scene 2, looks forward to his forthcoming meeting with Bérénice. It is almost a rehearsal of lines: 'Pourrai-je, sans trembler, lui dire: "Je vous aime?"' (l. 20). Lines 38–46 are an address to Bérénice of what he would like to say to her and represents the essence of his much longer speech in lines 210–258. Titus too has to rehearse his lines. It is rather the naked confrontation with Bérénice that disturbs him since he is now left without the intermediary of Antiochus who has already prepared the queen for what he is about to say. This does not make it easier for the emperor: 'Pourrai-je dire enfin: "Je ne veux plus vous voir?"' (l. 998). He too goes through the arguments that he must present to Bérénice in order to justify his action (l. 1027 sq). But they do not actually emerge in this way when he faces the queen in person.

I have remarked that in the case of Antigone the soliloquy serves to provide space for the characters to consider their future strategy. With Antigone, however, it does not have any specific consequences for speech. In other plays of Racine, characters are more conscious of what needs to be said. *Bérénice* is a case in point. Roxane too, even though she now has proof of Bajazet's betrayal in the letter he has sent to Atalide, wishes to hear it from his own lips:

> Poussons à bout l'ingrat, et tentons la fortune;
> Voyons si, par mes soins sur le trône élevé,
> Il osera trahir l'amour qui l'a sauvé. (ll. 1238–40)

Mithridate on two occasions creates the conditions of future dialogue with Monime when he decides to set her a trap. The first time he succeeds, but the next time the strategy rebounds upon him. Thésée, frustrated at his inability to pierce the mystery of what has occurred in Trézène, commands: 'Je veux de tout le crime être mieux éclairci' (l. 1459).

No doubt many of the features of the Racinian soliloquy I have highlighted may be constituent elements of the soliloquy in general, except that Racinian characters seem to pay more attention at an explicit level to problems of speech and listening. But Racine's use of the soliloquy seems to reflect the place of the character in the overall structure of the conditions of speech in the plays. Almost without exception those characters who have soliloquies are in some way isolated from discourse. Axiane can no longer speak with Porus and can only utter the words she should have spoken to him in isolation. They are consequently without effect:

> Mais que sert de pousser des soupirs superflus
> Qui se perdent en l'air et que tu n'entends plus? (ll. 991–92)

Hermione and Oreste are the two characters accorded soliloquies in *Andromaque.* She has been abandoned by Pyrrhus while he is eventually abandoned by Hermione and made a pariah because of the assassination.

Although Axiane can recreate a presence in her soliloquy, this particular form of speech most often represents a dialogue without presence which underlines the eventual isolation of the characters. In speaking the words to himself before seeing Bérénice, Antiochus foreshadows that isolation he will suffer in the ensuing dialogue. She firmly suggests to him that, in the name of friendship, what he has said to her will be instantly forgotten (264–65). Mithridate's status as the only character accorded a soliloquy in the tragedy further isolates him from discourse, since Monime has rejected him for his own son:

> Tout m'abandonne ailleurs, tout me trahit ici!
> Pharnace, amis, maîtresse, et toi, mon fils aussi. (ll. 1013–14)

Indeed his speech in Act IV, scene 5 could be said to have no place in any dialogue with another character in the play because Arbate has already sided with Xipharès (it is significant that Arcas brings the poison to Monime and Arbate knocks it from her hand). Clytemnestre too suffers exclusion from dialogue in that she is unable to get near to Agamemnon for long enough in order to uncover the truth:

> Et pourquoi me cacher? et par quelle injustice
> Faut-il que sur mon front sa honte rejaillisse? (ll. 825–26)

Phèdre learns that she is rejected by Hippolyte. He has not heard her because he is in love with Aricie. Roxane, however, for a brief moment, attempts to escape from the isolation represented by the duplicity of Atalide and the treachery of Bajazet, on the slender grounds that Atalide may be mistaken in believing that Bajazet loves her:

> N'importe. Poursuivons. Elle peut comme moi
> Sur des gages trompeurs s'assurer de sa foi. (ll. 1227–28)

She is prepared to give dialogue one last chance. Her belief is however a further illusion in the way some Racinian characters approach speech.

So, the central impact of Racinian speech lies not in its status as a conveyor of plot or as a descriptive account of passion and character. Speech in itself constitutes an event either in its production or its postponement, for the problems of speech are a constant element in the characters' concerns. Speech is at all times an unwanted and unwelcome commitment, a commitment which is encapsulated in a single moment of time, or in a series of moments which represent the unrelenting momentum of the tragic action. The characters reflect then, at the level of the content of speech itself and with intense awareness, on all aspects of the communicative situation in which they find themselves.

Chapter 3
Language, Voice and Substitution

From the general grounds and conditions of discourse, I passed in the previous chapter to a discussion of the way in which certain aspects of speech are productive in themselves of tragic action, and an essential component of that tragedy of speech was found to be the tension of utterance. That tension was situated in the context of performance, other aspects of which I should now like to explore. First, on a number of occasions, a substitution of voice takes place where one character has to perform in the place of another. In one sense, the form of voice substitution in which one character 'borrows' the voice of another who acts as a messenger will become a further reflection on the characters' desire sometimes to avoid confrontation with others, thus reinforcing the point I have made regarding the imperative relationship between seeing and speaking. As one might expect, the transfer of voice from one character to another is not, as we shall see, without its complications which are themselves capable of generating tragic action.

But I should like to take the idea of voice substitution further and explore its occurrence this time not between but within characters. A single character can often be composed of a number of voices which are not all appropriate to the circumstances in which they find themselves. This is not to say that the concept of voice represents a purely pragmatic choice, although certainly strategy is not far from the characters' thoughts. But voice becomes a mode of being, where the characters are or become what they are through the speech they perform, especially in relation to others for whom their interlocutors are what they hear. This perspective helps to raise a number of issues related to the notion of 'character' in itself and authenticity, a notion crucial to the exploration of the communicative situation in Racinian tragedy. It will also allow us to reflect on the concept of unity and continuity within a character's speech, and therefore within the concept of character itself.

Let us begin with the form of voice substitution which operates between characters, one of whom, as the messenger of the other, conveys the *voice* of the message-giver. Racine's tragedies contain a number of messengers. For example, Arcas is despatched to meet up with Clytemnestre and Iphigénie in an attempt to turn them away from Aulis. Oreste acts as a messenger for the Greeks and, later, for Hermione. Antiochus conveys a message for Titus. Œnone accepts to speak to

Thésée and lies to save her mistress. Substitution is often marked by the phrase 'par ma voix' or 'par votre voix'. Oreste tells Pyrrhus: 'Avant que tous les Grecs vous parlent par ma voix' (l. 143), and Agrippine recognises Burrhus' status as a messenger for Néron when she complains:

> Je vous entends: Néron m'apprend par votre voix
> Qu'en vain Britannicus s'assure sur mon choix. (ll. 245–46)

The most exalted sort of messenger is one who acts for a deity. The deity speaks with a human voice. There are two occasions when such a substitution is in potential only, or in the form of a desire. Esther pleads that God should lend her his voice (l. 289) and in *Athalie* Josabet asks that God speak through Joas during his interview with Athalie. In the pagan world, it is Calchas in *Iphigénie* who speaks for the gods. The case of Joad is more complex. Initially he acts as an intermediary:

> Avant que son destin s'explique par ma voix,
> Je vais l'offrir au Dieu par qui règnent les rois. (ll. 177–78)

Joad gradually, however, seems to embody the voice of God:

> Mais d'où vient que mon cœur frémit d'un saint effroi?
> Est-ce l'esprit divin qui s'empare de moi?
> C'est lui-même! il m'échauffe, il parle; mes yeux s'ouvrent,
> Et les siècles obscurs devant moi se découvrent. (ll. 1129–32)

But the messenger's task is not simply one of quotation. It carries with it certain responsibilities. The messenger must ensure that the message is conveyed accurately, and in the tone required. The messenger must recreate or even replicate, the original, since the message-giver has handed over control of his voice to the messenger. The content *and* manner of the original must therefore coincide. Agamemnon makes it quite clear that Arcas adopt his own voice and 'speak as one' with him (in this case, the king's voice is contained in a letter): 'Et que ta voix s'accorde avec ce que j'écris'. (l. 143) Phèdre may well argue that Œnone's voice, as the conveyor of a message to Hippolyte, will be more effective but, in advising Œnone how to speak to him, she makes it clear that the adopted voice must be as if it were that of Phèdre:

> Tes discours trouveront plus d'accès que les miens;
> Presse, pleure, gémis, plains-lui Phèdre mourante,
> Ne rougis point de prendre une voix suppliante. (ll. 808–10)

The message that must be conveyed to Thésée is, on the other hand, of a different order. Œnone must use exclusively her own voice, and she therefore stipulates that she will speak to Thésée only on condition that Phèdre remain silent (l. 894), especially in view of the fact the words that Œnone speaks in lines 1014–22 are entirely of her own invention. The fiction of Phèdre as the message-giver is however maintained because Œnone explains to Thésée the reason for Phèdre not speaking herself: 'Phèdre épargnait plutôt un père redoutable' (l. 1001), thus echoing Hippolyte's own reasons for keeping silent.

That bearing a message is an act of some complexity is further illustrated by the case of Atalide in *Bajazet*. Acomat sees her situation in fairly straightforward terms: speaking of the relationship he has engineered between Roxane and Bajazet, he remarks to Osmin:

> Du prince en apparence elle (=Atalide) reçoit les vœux,
> Mais elle les reçoit pour les rendre à Roxane. (ll. 102–3)

Atalide herself understands her position as being the go-between where:

> Roxane, se livrant tout entière à ma foi,
> Du cœur de Bajazet se reposait sur moi,
> M'abandonnait le soin de tout ce qui le touche,
> Le voyait par mes yeux, lui parlait par ma bouche. (ll. 347–50)

Clearly problems arise in this instance as to the exact nature of the transaction when we realise that Atalide and Bajazet are in love and practising a massive deception on Roxane. It may well be that Atalide has informed Bajazet exactly of Roxane's words but she cannot at the same time 'speak as one' with Roxane, unless the words spoken by Roxane were those she herself would use in conveying her own love for Bajazet.

What, however, about the message in the other direction? In this case, the voices of Bajazet and Atalide have spoken consecutively: 'Je l'ai pressé de feindre, et j'ai parlé pour lui' (l. 388). One might expect that an exact convergence had been achieved. But it turns out that Atalide has been obliged to explain Bajazet's words in a more favourable light:

> Car enfin Bajazet ne sait point se cacher.
> Je connais sa vertu prompte à s'effaroucher.
> Il faut qu'à tous moments, tremblante et secourable,
> Je donne à ses discours un sens plus favorable. (ll. 391–94)

The message here is a form of substitution which takes place at the same time (and in the same place) as the message-giver himself speaks. It is not the replication of an original as such.

Messengers are not always willing messengers. It is a function that is often endured. Oreste finds himself in this position twice, once when Pyrrhus asks him to convey to Hermione the news that he will marry her after all (ll. 623–34), and the second time when Hermione insists that Pyrrhus should know that she is the reason for his assassination (ll. 1267–70). This particular message does not get through. There are times too when the role of messenger is imposed. Néron can be seen in this light, at least the Néron before the abduction of Junie. He is perceived as the messenger of his mother, as he explains to her in Act IV, scene 2:

> Le sénat chaque jour et le peuple, irrités
> De s'ouïr par ma voix dicter vos volontés ... (ll. 1231–32)

However, at the beginning of the play, Agrippine perceives Néron as the messenger of others:

> En public, à mon heure, on me donne audience:
> Sa réponse est dictée, et même son silence. (ll. 119–20)

In both instances, Néron is regarded as having no voice of his own. The action can thus be understood as an attempt on the part of Néron to become a message-giver in his own right, and his power over Junie (power can be seen as power over another's voice) allows him to achieve that status. Junie is a messenger in two senses. In the first, she signals to Agrippine that her own power as the message-giver is finished. In the second, she actually relays a message to Britannicus 'dictated' by Néron who advises her on the precise manner in which she is to carry out her task:

> De son bannissement prenez sur vous l'offense,
> Et soit par vos discours, soit par votre silence,
> Du moins par vos froideurs, faites-lui concevoir
> Qu'il doit porter ailleurs ses vœux et son espoir. (ll. 671–74)

This is the case of a message where, while it is in one way carried out, (that is to say that Junie attempts to display only 'froideur' to Britannicus), the messenger and the message-giver can never 'speak as one', as Néron soon understands. It illustrates also the degree to which the message-giver can never be in complete control of the message or the messenger.

Bérénice provides another particularly complex instance of voice substitution. Titus seems to perceive no difficulty in the task he gives to Antiochus: 'Et je veux simplement emprunter votre voix' (l. 694). At this stage Titus is obviously unaware that Antiochus has been, and still is, in love with Bérénice, so that his confidence in Antiochus is based on the close friendship he thinks binds them all together as a trio:[1]

> Je sais que Bérénice, à vos soins redevables,
> Croit posséder en vous un ami véritable.
> Elle ne voit dans Rome et n'écoute que vous;
> Vous ne faites qu'un cœur et qu'une âme avec nous. (ll. 695–98)

Titus's perception of the situation is anticipated by Bérénice in the first act after Antiochus has broken the silence imposed upon him by the Palestinian queen:

> Cent fois je me suis fait une douceur extrême
> D'entretenir Titus dans un autre lui-même. (ll. 271–72)

The irony of the situation is therefore that in one sense Titus and Antiochus are considered interchangeable, and that Antiochus has spoken as if at one with them. (Interestingly, Phénice harbours the sentiment that Antiochus is a possible substitute for Titus especially when, as she reminds her mistress, the emperor has yet to confirm their marriage (l. 289 and ll. 293–97).) But there is a further irony in that Antiochus, in conveying the message entrusted to him by Titus, uses not his own voice, but that of the man she loves. By means of the substitution of voice, Antiochus 'becomes' Titus. In achieving that position, on the other hand, he merely repeats the situation of rejection he has already found himself in with Bérénice in Act I, scene 4. Being another Titus is of no advantage to him whatsoever.

Voice substitution in *Bajazet* too offers Racine the opportunity to promote a number of ironies. The situation at the primary level of substitution is that Atalide is the intermediary between Bajazet and Roxane, the latter being led to believe that Bajazet's expressions of love for her are genuine. Atalide is thus the voice of both Roxane and Bajazet. A problem occurs when Roxane wishes to dispense with mediation and to hear Bajazet himself:

> Je ne vous presse point de vouloir aujourd'hui
> Me prêter votre voix pour m'expliquer à lui:
> Je veux que devant moi sa bouche et son visage
> Me découvrent son cœur sans me laisser d'ombrage,

> Que lui-même, en secret amené dans ces lieux,
> Sans être préparé se présente à mes yeux. (ll. 327–32)

The withdrawal of the intermediary immediately exposes Bajazet who himself does not possess the necessary voice to deal with the situation. After all Bajazet has not spoken with the voice Roxane requires. This function has been performed by Atalide herself, and her 'interpretation' of his love has stood for his voice. For this reason, it is significant that before this point (Act I, scene 4) Bajazet himself has not been introduced into the action. He appears in the first scene of Act II when he must speak in the manner that Roxane has been led to expect that he will. He must construct a voice which will substitute for his own, but in so doing he must speak at one with Atalide (an irony in itself) but also with Roxane's expectations. This loss of a voice is marked most strongly in Act II, scene 5, when Atalide's anger at Bajazet's attitude leads her to withdraw her mediation of her own accord, to which Bajazet can only answer: 'Eh bien! Mais quels discours faut-il que je lui tienne?' (l. 786)

The situation is to a certain extent reversed at a later stage of the action when, from being the messenger, Atalide requires a messenger herself. After Act III, scene 5, Bajazet and Atalide no longer meet. Having learnt by means of a letter from Bajazet that he has now decided to reveal the truth to Roxane, she sends Zaïre to persuade the prince that he must save his life. She in fact regrets that her voice is no longer available to help him, that he can no longer speak through her:

> Que ne puis-je moi-même,
> Echauffant par mes pleurs ses soins trop languissants,
> Mettre dans ses discours tout l'amour que je sens! (ll. 1158–60)

Roxane views the whole situation of deceit from a different, almost the reverse, perspective. It is rather her love for Bajazet, conveyed by Atalide, which has allowed Atalide to express real feelings of love for the prince: 'N'aurais-je tout tenté que pour une rivale?' (l.1072). Roxane herself has acted as the intermediary:

> Ardente elle veillait aux soins de mon amour,
> Et c'est moi qui du sien ministre trop fidèle
> Semble depuis six mois ne veiller que pour elle. (l.1213)

The removal of the intermediary voice creates problems in other Racinian tragedies. Joas is immediately exposed to danger when Athalie removes the possibility of Josabet answering her questions on his behalf (ll. 626–27), except that his own voice is imbued with the teaching of his substitute parents, as Athalie herself is quick to recognise (l. 690). Indeed, an interesting situation develops at the end of *Bérénice* when it seems that the dialogue has come to an impasse, especially now that Titus is aware that Antiochus is a rival in love. His intermediary has been exposed as someone with an ulterior motive. How is speech to resume? Titus has been unable to be resolute in his decision to be an emperor instead of a lover (he like Bérénice has threatened suicide) and now Antiochus too will take refuge in death (ll. 1459–60). Not only has the voice of the messenger failed as a strategy, but Titus's own voice has failed as well. Dialogue as a whole has collapsed. There is no intermediary who can re-engage them in speech with each other. It falls to Bérénice to reunite them in a speech addressed to them but to which they are unable to respond.

The end of *Phèdre* also revolves around the withdrawal or death of all those who are in a position to 'mediate' with Thésée and to reveal the truth, that is to say, to substitute their own voice for that of Phèdre. Aricie refuses to divulge Hippolyte's secret, as he has forbidden her to do and she in fact removes herself from Thésée's presence for fear of giving herself away. The king then learns of the death of Œnone who has acted as Phèdre's messenger. Finally, Théramène appears in order to recount the ghastly death of Hippolyte. Racine's dramatic purpose in all this is to expose more and more the voice of Phèdre as the only source left able to reveal the truth (strangely Théramène is at no point considered as performing this function). Phèdre can no longer hide behind a substitute. She must assume the responsibility of speaking which she had devolved to Œnone, and that is a solitary task.

So far I have considered the messenger acting for the message-giver. In the examples I have explored, the terms of the message, whether willingly or unwillingly conveyed, have been clear to the messenger. I should now like to turn to a category of substitution where voice is usurped, that is to say where characters speak in the place of rather than on behalf of others. Usurpation as a form of substitution means that speech is addressed by and to characters it should not be. Equally meetings happen which should not have done.

It might seem odd to think of Hippolyte in terms of a usurper, but this is precisely what he is in Act II, scene 2 of *Phèdre* when Hippolyte confronts Aricie for the first time in the play. The young prince assumes on this occasion the voice of power in that he liberates Aricie from the harsh régime imposed on her by Thésée who has ruled that no man must fall in love with her:

> Je puis vous affranchir d'une austère tutelle.
> Je révoque des lois dont j'ai plaint la rigueur. (ll. 474–75)

In a sense, Hippolyte simply fills a power vacuum left by Thésée after his death has been announced. But it is not perhaps as simple as that, since it is obvious that Hippolyte has not agreed with his father's actions and takes the first opportunity to countermand them. He therefore usurps the voice of the king. Usurpation means that 'speaking as one' is precluded from the start. Hippolyte is quite conscious of reversing a situation created by Thésée's family:

> Je vous cède, ou plutôt je vous rends une place,
> Un sceptre que jadis vos aïeux ont reçu
> De ce fameux mortel que la terre a conçu.
> L'adoption le mit entre les mains d'Egée.
> Athènes, par mon père accrue et protégée,
> Reconnut avec joie un roi si généreux,
> Et laissa dans l'oubli vos frères malheureux.
> Athènes dans ses murs maintenant vous rappelle. (ll. 494–501)

On the political level this is a scene which should not have taken place. But the scene is actually made possible through another type of displacement, this time within an individual character, since Hippolyte has discovered a new voice. As the ferocious hunter of legend, he has ignored women. Love now provides Hippolyte with a voice in which, however clumsily, he can communicate with Aricie. The voice of power is also a voice of love, rather than the voice of enmity that his father represents. In other plays the voice of love is so often associated with the voice of tyranny. This variety of voices within an individual character will be explored more fully at a later stage.

Hippolyte, however, also usurps the place of his father in his meeting with Phèdre but this time unwillingly and at her instigation. Phèdre speaks words of love to Hippolyte which should have been directed at, or at least preserved for, Thésée. This is tellingly illustrated in the scene where she declares her love to Hippolyte himself and begins by failing to distinguish between father and son (ll.634–44). Gradually, Hippolyte becomes more and more the subject of Phèdre's speech to the extent that he displaces his father as the object of discourse. Hippolyte, through the voice of Phèdre, usurps the place of his father. An interesting variation on the theme of usurpation and displacement occurs later in the play at Phèdre's discovery that Hippolyte is in fact in love with Aricie. Phèdre can 'hear' the voice that she feels should have been directed at her:

> Au moment que je parle, ah! mortelle pensée!
> Ils bravent la fureur d'une amante insensée.
> Malgré ce même exil qui va les écarter,
> Ils font mille serments de ne se point quitter. (ll. 1253–56)

Aricie has thus usurped her own place as Hippolyte's interlocutor, a purely fanciful notion, of course.

But another voice substitution occurs at the end of the play which echoes Hippolyte's meeting with Aricie in Act II, scene 2. Thésée adopts Aricie as his daughter and restores communication with Aricie, since she is no longer the excluded person she once was. Hippolyte has been the first to reestablish this communication, in which case Thésée 'usurps' or at least replaces the voice of Hippolyte. The father becomes the substitute for the son. Moreover, the king also validates the earlier act of usurpation on the part of Hippolyte who had freed Aricie from her chains.

This usurpation of language is not of course limited to *Phèdre.* It occurs in a complex way in *Bajazet.* Not only does Roxane speak to Bajazet as she should to Amurat, but Atalide usurps the language of Roxane in order to pursue her own love of Bajazet. In *Mithridate* the offers of marriage made by the two sons to Monime displace the 'legitimate' offer of marriage made by Mithridate. Indeed he later accuses Monime, at the same time mistaking the real culprit, of listening favourably to other declarations of love:

> Je vois qu'un fils perfide, épris de vos beautés,
> Vous a parlé d'amour, et que vous l'écoutez. (ll. 589–90)

This usurpation of language is sometimes underlined by direct quotation of what should have been said to another. Pyrrhus, in leading Andromaque to the altar, is quoted by Oreste as having declared:

> "Je vous donne [...] ma couronne et ma foi!
> Andromaque, régnez sur Epire et sur moi." (ll. 1507–8)

The line would scan perfectly if 'Andromaque' were replaced by 'Hermione', to whom Pyrrhus had originally promised marriage. Cléone is acutely conscious of the situation and points out the irony to Hermione:

> Il l'épouse, il lui donne, avec son diadème,
> La foi que vous venez de recevoir vous-même. (ll. 1137–38)

Substitution as usurpation is further enhanced if characters meet each other when they should not do so. In these instances space itself is usurped. In general terms, the relation between space and substitution is articulated by Agrippine. I have remarked that the whole dynamic of the action in *Britannicus* is determined by the need on the part of Néron to find a voice, and that this is in some way resolved by the relationship Néron seeks with Junie where his 'voice' can take on an independence of its own. After all, Octavie has been imposed on him by his mother. Agrippine perceives the situation in spatial terms when she remarks to Albine:

> Bientôt, si je ne romps ce funeste lien,
> Ma place est occupée, et je ne suis plus rien. (ll. 881–82)

If we remember that she 'occupies' Néron's space by dictating what he should say (see ll. 1231–32), her displacement represents in fact a loss of voice and the occupation of her space. Agrippine is thus marginalised, as is evident in having twice to speak with Burrhus the substitute instead of with the emperor himself. She is also waiting at his door:

> Faut-il que vous veniez attendre son réveil?
> Qu'errant dans le palais sans suite et sans escorte,
> La mère de César veille seule à sa porte? (ll. 3–5)

Certainly, in Act IV, Agrippine manages to occupy a more central space, but is yet again, in Act V, relegated to the margins while the real action, the murder of Britannicus, takes place in an adjacent room. Her own speech is thus rendered marginal. In a similar way, Néron occupies the place of Britannicus, not only in terms of the throne, but in terms of the voice which speaks to Junie. It is natural therefore that Néron should react violently when Britannicus re-establishes his rightful place in Act III, scene 7.

Another interesting case where voice substitution of a sort is underlined by scenic presentation occurs in *Andromaque.* In Act III, scene 6, Pyrrhus patently expects to encounter Hermione, having now supposedly renounced his love for Andromaque. The meeting is announced at the very end of Act II, when Phoenix advises Pyrrhus to see Hermione, presumably to confirm their marriage. Hermione is on stage for three scenes of Act III, arriving in Act III, scene 2 when she encounters Oreste. Nothing in fact suggests, either in this or the following scene, that she expects to see Pyrrhus. Instead she is approached by Andromaque who pleads for help in saving her son. Hermione dismisses Andromaque scornfully and leaves. After a brief scene of four lines between Andromaque and Céphise, Pyrrhus enters expecting to encounter Hermione, as his first two lines indicate:

Où donc est la princesse?
Ne m'avais-tu pas dit qu'elle était en ces lieux? (ll. 890–91)

To this Phoenix can only reply: 'Je le croyais' (l. 892). Who should be there but the very person Phoenix has been persuading Pyrrhus to abandon? The consequence of this remarkable series of events (did Hermione forget that Pyrrhus was coming or was she not expecting him? — in either case the irony is acute) is that Pyrrhus speaks words to Andromaque that should have been directed at Hermione, that is to say, he makes a promise of marriage. Andromaque has usurped, however unwittingly, the place of Hermione as the character to whom crucial words should have been addressed.

Considerations of space are paramount in any analysis of the theme of substitution in *Bérénice*. In the first scene Antiochus introduces Arsace to 'ce cabinet superbe et solitaire' which 'des secrets de Titus est le dépositaire' (ll. 3–4):

C'est ici quelquefois qu'il se cache à sa cour,
Lorsqu'il vient à la reine expliquer son amour.
De son appartement cette porte est prochaine,
Et cet autre conduit dans celui de la reine. (ll. 5–8)

Arsace is then despatched to fetch the queen from her own apartment. The 'cabinet' is clearly defined as a space of intimacy where Titus and Bérénice have spoken to each other of their love every day. Antiochus, in declaring his love to the queen, usurps not only the words which Bérénice is awaiting from Titus but, in a sense, Titus's space. Now, Antiochus has participated in conversations with Titus and Bérénice before the action of the play begins, although it is not stated where those conversations have taken place. We must assume that they too have occurred in the space represented in the play, otherwise Antiochus would not be aware of the transgression constituted by his presence there. In any case, Bérénice herself is not surprised to find him near her apartment.

But the conversations between the three of them that have preceded the action of the play have been of another sort. On these occasions, Titus and Bérénice have believed that they have all spoken as one, since Titus has regarded Antiochus as another version of himself (without perceiving the irony that this entails). There has been no usurpation but unity. The moment Antiochus breaks the silence imposed on him by the Palestinian queen, he disturbs that unity. He becomes a rival again, rather than the friend he has pretended to be (see l.26). He speaks words that, in that particular space, belong exclusively to Titus. Concomitantly, Bérénice hears words in a space where she expects them to be enunciated by Titus. Indeed, Act III, scene 3, continues this spatial irony. Antiochus has come to deliver lines that are indeed those of Titus, since Titus has asked Antiochus to act as his substitute in conveying to the queen the news that she must leave Rome. In this case Antiochus cannot be said to be usurping Titus's space as he is speaking 'at one' with him. The reaction of Bérénice is again to a certain extent determined by what has hitherto been associated with that space, although she also believes the messenger to be suspect.[2]

So far I have dealt with the concept of substitution between characters, both at the level of the messenger and at the level of usurpation. I should now like to turn to the issue of substitution where it occurs within a character. In Racinian tragedy, a single character cannot always be construed as possessing one voice and may use, at various stages of the action, a variety of different voices. This discontinuity is evident on a number of occasions. One can think of many instances when Racinian characters go back on what they have said on previous occasions. A change of mind requires a different voice. There is a world of difference between Pyrrhus's first interview with Oreste and his second. Andromaque herself in fact provides a number of problems in the different ways she speaks to Pyrrhus at certain moments of the play. Hermione's voice too changes starkly in the course of one scene. This perspective leads to some rather crucial considerations concerning the relationship between voice and character, between voice and self within individual characters. Is the discontinuity I have referred to simply a variation of a 'core' self, in which case we must identify that voice which represents it and which acts as a sort of measure by which we can understand other voices of the same character? Or does this discontinuity manifest a succession of selves where the self is the equivalent of a mode of speech? Is voice, in other words, a mode of being?

The characters themselves seem to be aware of their own voices as presenting a discontinuity. Pyrrhus, in excusing the position he had adopted in Act I, scene 2, explains to Oreste that: 'A moi-même, en un mot, je devenais contraire' (l. 610). What is this 'moi-même' to which he refers? It must exist objectively, as more than a mere subjective perception, because it is recognised by Phoenix who, when commenting on Pyrrhus's stance in Act II, scene 4, exclaims:

Ah! je vous reconnais; et ce juste courroux,
Ainsi qu'à tous les Grecs, Seigneur, vous rend à vous. (ll. 627–28)

Pyrrhus's voice with Andromaque is clearly reckoned to be a different one from that of the hero of Troy.[3] The coming and going of Pyrrhus between Andromaque and Hermione is thus reflected at the level of dialogue by his adoption of one voice or another. Clearly the hero of Troy has yielded to the suitor of Andromaque. Which is the real Pyrrhus? Does such a 'character' exist? Is Pyrrhus merely the sum of his various voices? Similarly, it is interesting that at the beginning of Act III Pylade should say to Oreste: 'Je ne vous connais plus; vous n'êtes plus vous–même' (l. 710). Hermione too expects a different Oreste from the one who has just spoken to her in Act II, scene 2: 'Attendais-tu, Cléone, un courroux si modeste?' (l. 833). In what way, then, is voice a marker of recognition by others?[4] In what way is it a marker of recognition for the self since the self does not always recognise itself in the voice that is speaking? Hermione in Act V, scene 1 of *Andromaque* is a classic case in point. Her speech in this scene emphasises the full significance of her words to Oreste later in the same act:

Ah! fallait-il en croire une amante insensée?
Ne devais pas-tu lire au fond de ma pensée? (ll. 1545–45)

Which self did he hear? Which should he have heard? How could he have known? Is voice an important (or adequate) way of knowing people?[5]

Titus's need to substitute one voice for another, in other words to adopt another mode of performance, is determined by his elevation to the status of emperor and by his recognition that Rome will not accept a queen as his wife. The whole action of *Bérénice* revolves around Titus's difficulty in expressing this to the queen herself. It is as if his accession produces a new self, or at least an abandonment of a former self:

Je connus que bientôt, loin d'être à ce que j'aime,
Il fallait, cher Paulin, renoncer à moi-même. (ll. 463–64)

The voice of the lover must give way to the voice of the emperor, the latter demanding that he say:'"Partez, et ne me voyez plus"' (l. 522), thus substituting for that voice which conveyed, according to Bérénice, 'ses serments redoublés mille fois' (l. 173). The very need to rehearse this voice, however, suggests that he is not yet sure of it (see also l.998). What is ironic in Titus's personal history is that this is not the first substitution of self. Bérénice has transformed him from debauchery to heroism (see ll. 511–18). But this change did not produce the 'emperor' but a more devoted lover anxious to please his loved one. It is not yet a voice emancipated from Bérénice. The voice of the emperor, which accompanies his recognition of his responsibilities, is his own discovery. But Titus has difficulties in disentangling one voice from the other. The voice of the lover is still inscribed within the voice of the emperor. This is the reason why Titus uses Antiochus as a messenger.

That the self is associated with voice is emphasised by the example of Antiochus. Before meeting with Bérénice in Act I, scene 4, he asks himself:

> Eh bien, Antiochus, es-tu toujours le même?
> Pourrai-je, sans trembler, lui dire: "Je vous aime"? (ll. 19–20)

The voice in which he has conversed with Titus and Bérénice (who have valued him as a friend) has been a false voice which he has had to construct in order to conceal his true feelings. In any case, we can see through Antiochus the degree to which the self ('toi-même') is associated with the need to speak, to adopt a voice, to adopt a different mode of being.

As I have suggested, the characters themselves recognise that they speak with a different voice, that they substitute one voice for another. The link of voice with the self is clear in the case of Hippolyte. In Act II, scene 2, having said more than he had intended in speaking to Aricie, he exclaims in anguish: 'Par quel trouble me vois-je emporté loin de moi?' (l. 536) He further describes to Aricie the change that has come over him:

> Moi-même, pour tout fruit de mes soins superflus,
> Maintenant je me cherche et ne me trouve plus.
> Mon arc, mes javelots, mon char, tout m'importune;
> Je ne me souviens plus des leçons de Neptune;
> Mes seuls gémissements font retentir les bois,
> Et mes coursiers oisifs ont oublié ma voix. (ll. 547–52)

He relates his new self directly to voice, or at least to the loss of his former voice. That a new voice is at a stage of potential is recognised by Ismène before Hippolyte meets Aricie:[6]

> Le nom d'amant peut-être offense son courage;
> Mais il en a les yeux, s'il n'en a le langage. (ll. 413–14)

We of course already know that Hippolyte has passed from the potential stage of the language of love to the actual stage. Hippolyte's recognition of what is happening to him is marked by his attempt to deny it:

> Ami, qu'oses-tu dire?
> Toi qui connais mon cœur depuis que je respire,
> Des sentiments d'un cœur si fier, si dédaigneux,
> Peux-tu me demander le désaveu honteux? (ll. 65–68)

Théramène is only too well aware of the transformation under way: 'Mais que sert d'affecter un superbe discours?' (l. 127) But in this opening scene Hippolyte is caught between two voices, the former voice which represents action and the new one which reduces him to immobility. The old voice talks about pursuing monsters at the same time as betraying the impossibility of that discourse now that he is in love.[7] But the old voice disappears from Act II, scene II when he speaks to Aricie. The new voice of love takes over completely and displaces all others. Hippolyte becomes another.

Other characters experience a new mode of being through the discovery of an alternative voice. Monime, for example, discovers a voice which for her is unprecedented in refusing to accede to Mithridate's threats:

> Mais le dessein est pris, rien ne peut m'ébranler.
> Jugez-en, puisque ainsi je vous ose parler, (ll. 1361–62)

Up to that point she has been a model of restraint, even to the point of encouraging Xipharès to abandon her so that she can obey the king. Mathan now speaks for Baal and no longer for the Jewish religion. His old voice is an embarrassment and even an object of guilt which can only be distinguished with the destruction of the temple (ll. 955–62). Athalie herself conveys a discontinuity of voice when her regal voice deserts her. That it has done so is clear in her outburst in Act II, scene 5: 'Je puis, quand je voudrai, parler en souveraine' (l. 592). But can she? This loss of voice is marked in the most fundamental way: we learn that on being ordered from the sacred confines of the temple by Joad: ' [...] sa langue en sa bouche à l'instant s'est glacée' (l. 411). She becomes moved by Joas and adopts the voice of the mother. She is no longer her 'self' and she has moved to another mode of being. Mathan knows this:

> Ami, depuis deux jours je ne la connais plus.
> Ce n'est plus cette reine éclairée, intrépide,
> Elevée au-dessus de son sexe timide. (ll. 870–72)

Athalie has lost her grip on power, so much associated with voice in Racine. Is the self only as consistent as the voice that conveys it?

The search for a self through voice is, however, most tellingly illustrated by the character of Néron. Whose voice will he adopt as emperor? The pressure is on him to abandon the position where he is seen merely as the mouthpiece of his mother and to speak independently. One problem is that his voice and that of his mother have been perceived as one, as Junie — the perfect 'naive' observer — recognises:

> Il (= Britannicus) m'aime; il obéit à l'empereur son père,
> Et j'ose dire encore, à vous, à votre mère:
> Vos désirs sont toujours si conformes aux siens. (ll. 559–61)

Britannicus provides a clear example of a new voice constituting a new self, a self which is differentiated from the self which coincides with the mother's. One might even say that it is a vocal rather than an umbilical chord which is broken in the play. Indeed the language of love is so important for the emperor precisely because it is a language in which he and his mother cannot speak as one. As the play progresses, Néron is faced with a choice: to adopt the voice proposed by Burrhus and become a good emperor, or to adopt the voice of tyranny in which he is already well practised. Racine obviously had no choice which voice Néron was ultimately to use, since it was imposed on the playwright by history. But *Britannicus* provides us with a fascinating example, through Racine's reconstruction of the character of Néron, of someone constructing a self, a mode of being, through language. Rather than language being seen as exteriorising some sort of inner being, language can be understood as a form of being in its own right. Language does not inhabit characters: it is the characters who inhabit language.

The importance of the theme of the self and voice is that the self is actualised through voice. The self is the voice, even though there may be variations of it. In a radical sense, therefore, our knowledge of the characters and the knowledge characters have of each other derives only from what they say. It is important to emphasise this if we are to understand the precise parameters of the term 'psychological' as it applies to the category of tragedy represented by Racine's plays. The relation of self to voice is particularly apparent in those cases where characters can be understood to have discovered new selves which are coterminous with new voices. The construction of the self, as I have argued in the case of Néron, happens through language, through the adoption of a voice.

However, there are times when it appears that language, or the need for a particular voice, prevents characters from being 'themselves'. They have to adopt a false mode of being. I have already referred to the example of Antiochus. Esther is unable to speak with her own voice to Assuérus because he does not know that she is Jewish. Agamemnon's position reminds us of the loss of regal voice suffered by Athalie. Eurybate reports that in the camp Calchas alone rules and that: 'Le roi de son pouvoir se voit dépossédé' (ll. 1621–23). Agamemnon's situation thus reflects the problem he has had at the level of voice where the voice of the king has been determined all along by Calchas's interpretation of the oracle. It could be argued that the voice of the king in the play is a borrowed voice anyway and that the Greeks are within their rights to deprive him of it if he does not sacrifice all to their well-being.

The problem of false modes of being through speech is encountered by the characters themselves, and it is in some way related to the tension of utterance I have explored in Chapter 2. Pyrrhus remarks to Hermione:

> Je ne viens point, armé d'un indigne artifice,
> D'un voile d'équité couvrir mon injustice.
> Il suffit que mon cœur me condamne tout bas,
> Et je soutiendrais mal ce que je ne crois pas. (ll. 1277–81)

His statement in fact contains many interesting issues related to rhetoric, but suffice it to say here that Pyrrhus believes himself incapable of selecting another voice at this stage because he does not believe it would be credible. In fact he cannot return to his former mode of being. Substitution of voice thus has much to do with being plausible. A problem of credibility of this sort arises with the character of Andromaque herself. Andromaque has, of course, always been a subject of controversy, especially as she appears in Act III, scene 6. A much more conciliatory, even flattering, Andromaque replaces the formerly proud and renunciatory character of Act I. The difficulty arises from the problem of voice, however, rather than at the so-called 'psychological' level, and in fact betrays a weakness in the rhetorical structure of the play. An Andromaque who would have remained faithful to her initial stance of refusal would not have allowed Racine to deploy the many effects he exploits in the coming and going of Pyrrhus to Hector's widow. The play would have turned out to be a sterile lament on the part of Pyrrhus. Hermione and Oreste would have remained in a rather static relationship to one another.

What Pyrrhus illustrates in Act IV, scene 5 is the difficulty of sustaining another voice. Hermione too is unable to disguise her true feelings for long, as is manifest in her first interview with Oreste when, on hearing

Oreste declare that, after all, Pyrrhus despises her, she asks him accusingly what exactly gives him that impression (ll. 550–54). Bajazet too is ill-equipped to adopt a false mode of being through speech. Atalide's concern at Roxane's demand to see Bajazet without her assistance underlines this inability: 'Car enfin Bajazet ne sait point se cacher' (l. 391). Indeed Bajazet decides in Act II, scene 5 that: 'Je ne puis plus tromper une amante incrédule' (l. 742). This may be a statement of intent, although he adds that:

> [...] ma bouche et mes yeux du mensonge ennemis,
> Peut-être, dans le temps que je voudrais lui plaire,
> Feraient par leur désordre un effet tout contraire. (ll. 744–46)

In Act II, scene 5 he finally chooses to tell the truth despite the fact that it will lead to his death (ll. 1008–10). Similarly Phèdre, in her fateful interview with Hippolyte, finds herself unable to keep up the voice of the mother (she is pleading for her son) and speaks instead as the incestuous adulteress. This is because the voice of the mother is a grafted voice, a pure strategy.

Sometimes the adoption of a false mode of being through speech is a deliberate act in that, as with Phèdre in the previous instance, it is essential that she find the voice which will be appropriate to the fate of her son. The need to adopt a different sort of voice occurs twice in *Mithridate* (I shall deal with the king himself at a later stage) where, on the first occasion, it is Monime who urges Xipharès to discover a stratagem by which he can leave Nymphée:

> Inventez des raisons qui puissent l'éblouir [...]
> Cherchez, Prince, cherchez, pour vous trahir vous-même,
> Tout ce que, pour jouir de leurs contentements,
> L'amour fait inventer aux vulgaires amants. (ll. 722–26)

It is the turn of Xipharès in Act IV, scene 2 to urge Monime to dissimulate: 'Feignez, efforcez-vous' (l. 1212). It is also true of course that, in Act I, scene 2 of *Andromaque*, Oreste is not anxious for his arguments to be too convincing and his representation of the Greeks' position is very stiff and uncommitted, his final speech indeed seeking the green light for approaching Hermione with his own desires in mind.

Many aspects of the preceding discussion point to a very real problem inherent in any communicative situation, particularly when speaking and listening are matters of life and death, and that is authenticity. What can we regard as the real self? If self is the equivalent of language, which language must be believed and acted upon? It may be that an essential element of Racinian tragedy is precisely that decisions must be made on the basis of the discontinuity of voice I have described. So the perception of vocal comportment or the understanding of any particular voice is crucial for the characters.

That there may be difficulties of perception is clearly recognised by Junie who questions whether Britannicus should believe the protestations of brotherly love made to him by Néron. The problem of perception is clearly one of recognition, whereby a character can readily identify inauthenticity, as the example of Britannicus demonstrates. Recognition of authenticity is made all the more difficult if the substitute voice is all that is heard and not the original. Roxane has to ask of Atalide: 'Mais m'en répondez-vous, vous qui parlez pour lui' (l. 268) She is able in fact to detect quite early in the play that Bajazet's voice does not ring true, given what she has been led to expect:

> Pourquoi faut-il au moins que, pour me consoler,
> L'ingrat ne parle pas comme on le fait parler. (ll. 275–76)

Atalide's voice has thus been more 'authentic' than Bajazet's. As Roxane again remarks: 'Vous parlez mieux pour lui qu'il ne parle lui-même' (l. 1058). Confirmation of this comes however only after the discovery of the letter on Atalide's person.

The issue of credibility is crucial for Oreste who for a moment is taken in by the conciliatory voice of Hermione. Oreste foresees the problem when Pylade informs him that on occasions Hermione has called on Oreste for help: 'Ah! si je le croyais' (l. 133). When confronted with her, he must decide what truth there is in her sympathy. It is a voice which he feels is not addressed to him. He knows ultimately that it is not the voice which she would like to adopt:

> Tout nous trahit, la voix, le silence, les yeux,
> Et les feux mal couverts n'en éclatent que mieux. (ll. 575–76)

It is a case of Hermione not being her 'self'.

A greater complication arises when a voice which is indeed genuine is perceived as otherwise. Antiochus suffers from the total incredulity of Bérénice when he simply conveys the message that Titus has given him. Even the stage space becomes inauthentic for Bérénice when she hears the emperor and not the lover speak in Act IV, scene 5:

> Tout cet appartement préparé par vos soins,
> Ces lieux, de mon amour si longtemps les témoins,

> Qui semblaient pour jamais me répondre du vôtre,
> Ces festons, où nos noms enlacés l'un dans l'autre,
> A mes tristes regards viennent partout s'offrir,
> Sont autant d'imposteurs que je ne puis souffrir. (ll. 1321–26)

There is no clearer indication of the way in which space in Racine is directly associated with voice. Hippolyte is another character whose voice is perceived as inauthentic when he conceals the truth rather than distorts it. Ironically, Thésée cannot understand how, in the countenance of an adulterer, there could '(briller) de la vertu le sacré caractère' (ll.1037–38). It is interesting therefore that Hippolyte should seek to convince Aricie of his sincerity in stopping at the temple where he will swear an eternal oath with her:

> Et tous les dieux enfin, témoins de mes tendresses,
> Garantiront la foi de mes saintes promesses. (ll. 1405–6)

A character may be responsible for producing a situation where a voice is heard as inauthentic, when actually the truth is being told. Agrippine threatens to reveal all the crimes that she has committed for her son. Burrhus informs her that she would simply not be believed:

> Madame, ils ne vous croiront pas.
> Ils sauront récuser l'injuste stratagème
> D'un témoin irrité qui s'accuse lui-même. (ll. 854–56)

It must be said that characters are not always successful in penetrating the falseness of a voice adopted by their interlocutors. Britannicus is a good example. Equally, we only see Roxane at the point where she begins to have doubts about Bajazet's sincerity. The best example of the failure to recognise inauthenticity is undoubtedly Monime in *Mithridate.* In Act III, scene 6 the king pretends to offer her the hand of Xipharès in marriage. After some initial doubts Monime finally accepts the offer as genuine:

> Mais enfin je vous crois, et je ne puis penser
> Qu'à feindre si longtemps vous puissiez vous forcer. (ll. 1097–98)

Of course Monime can only be persuaded if there are some grounds for believing what Mithridate is saying. Nonetheless Monime's example demonstrates, perhaps because of her own authenticity, a naive faith in taking language at its face value.

From the point of view of the spectator's perception of authenticity, a number of problems occur in seemingly innocent phrases. The characters' own expressions of sincerity are particularly noteworthy. Andromaque says curiously in Act IV, scene 1: 'Ce n'est point avec toi que mon cœur se déguise' (l. 1074), which perhaps suggests on occasions that Andromaque is capable of adopting a voice of disguise. A similar (but less curious) instance is Agrippine's remark to her son in Act IV, scene 2: 'C'est le sincère aveu que je voulais vous faire' (l. 1185). It most certainly implies that there have been occasions, which we can in fact easily imagine, when Agrippine has been less sincere.

A more interesting example is that of Monime in *Mithridate*. In the scene she shares with both brothers in Act I, scene 3, Monime replies to the overtures of Pharnace in the following way:

> Puis-je, laissant la feinte et les déguisements,
> Vous découvrir ici mes secrets sentiments? (ll. 245–46)

Does this imply that Monime is capable of deceit? Is the action of the play the very point at which Monime begins to be honest? But we know that Monime is capable of adopting another voice, as she demonstrates briefly in Act IV, scene 4 when she confronts Mithridate without revealing to him straightaway that she has discovered his treachery with her. It should be remembered that she urges Xipharès to 'invent' reasons which would take him away from Nymphée and her. Is Monime an example of an occasion in Racinian tragedy when inauthenticity is associated with a good end? It remains that Monime, seemingly a paragon of righteousness and modesty, is a more ambiguous case than we might imagine.

An even more surprising case, perhaps, is Burrhus. He steadfastly declares himself incapable of concealing the truth. Burrhus in fact possesses two voices, that of the honest old soldier and that of Néron's adviser and mouthpiece. He presents to Agrippine in Act I, scene 2 the former:

> Je répondrai, Madame, avec la liberté
> D'un soldat qui sait mal farder la vérité. (ll. 173–74)

Does this prevent Burrhus, on the other hand, from playing a role? After all he defends the abduction of Junie to the emperor's mother. Is this the voice of Burrhus or that of his master? Are we in any case really meant to believe that the abduction of Junie can be justified on political grounds (ll. 235–44)? Or is Burrhus covering for his master and adding his own gloss on the situation? Agrippine is in no doubt:

> Je vous entends: Néron m'apprend par votre voix
> Qu'en vain Britannicus s'assure de mon choix. (ll. 245–4)

It is perhaps shocking to hear the voice of the old soldier validating an act which will be presented to us later in rather different, more sinister terms. The problem is compounded by the fact that in Act III, scene 2 Burrhus shows himself to be more than aware of the real reasons for the abduction and speaks to Néron with as much of a voice of reproach as he dare. But he is still not prepared to concede to Agrippine as far on in the action as Act III, scene 3 that Néron is at fault: 'L'empereur n'a rien fait qu'on ne puisse excuser' (l. 822). Burrhus is, when confronted with Agrippine, a classic example of the 'official' voice.

Of course there are two advisers in *Britannicus*, Burrhus and Narcisse. It would be interesting therefore to explore the relationship of Néron's voice to that of Narcisse. In Act II, scene 1 we see Néron with both advisers ordering the banishment of Pallas. With which of these advisers do we associate this decisiveness? It is likely to be Narcisse, since it is from him that information concerning the conspiracy around Pallas emerges: he has learnt it himself from Britannicus. But is the decisive voice that of the emperor or that of Narcisse? It is true that Néron then ignores the voice of his adviser who urges him not to allow Junie and Britannicus to meet, even if it is for the purpose of conveying the cruel message that Néron has in mind (ll. 520–25). This is, however, Néron's mistake, as his reaction to the scene between the two lovers confirms. That the voice of Narcisse represents Néron's real voice can be seen from the fact that Narcisse has been actively engaged on the side of the emperor. He has been the accomplice of Néron's actions whereas the voice of Burrhus has provided what turns out to be a spurious public defence of those actions. Moreover, Burrhus justifies on two occasions Néron's *absence.* The voice of the emperor that Burrhus represents is a public voice, the voice of external justification, the voice that gives us a constructed version of the facts. Narcisse, on the other hand, represents the private voice, the voice of real motivation. Néron has to decide which of these voices will become his own. Racine seems to load the dice from the very start. How interesting that in Act V, scene 6 it should be natural that Narcisse speaks for Néron when he is confronted by his mother. Néron's search for a voice in the play is ultimately unsuccessful. He is reduced to repeating the word 'Junie': he has lost the source of his new found voice at the same time as losing that of his evil adviser.

Of course authenticity is not absent from the tragedies and performance cannot be related to deceit. Too often, the concentration on the destructive consequences of passion in Racinian tragedy can blind us to the very real values that survive the mayhem. Characters are certainly able to perceive authenticity in the voices of others. Athalie can recognise Joas's innocence in the way he speaks (ll. 629–630). Mathan is not so totally corrupt as to fail to acknowledge Josabet as a model of authenticity (ll. 1002–7). His corruption, however, is such that he will use her sincerity for his own purposes. Recognition of authenticity occurs also in *Esther.* Assuérus tells Esther:

> Oui, vos moindres discours ont des grâces secrètes;
> Une noble pudeur à tout ce que vous faites
> Donnent un prix que n'ont point ni le pourpre ni l'or.
> (ll. 1016–18)

Ironically, Assuérus makes this remark just before Esther reveals the truth of her situation to him. What this means is that Esther's voice is transparently authentic even though she has had to suppress the voice of the Israelite (kept alive in fact by the chorus). Another character who is incapable of adopting anything but an authentic voice is Junie, as Néron bitterly observes. At the very moment of conveying the message to Britannicus that Néron has given her, her authenticity shines through (ll. 747–48).

Since inauthenticity or insincerity, for whatever reason, are not uncommon among the characters, it is important that Racine should provide standards of authenticity in his plays which can act as a counterpoint to all that is inauthentic. Racine does not show us a humanity devoid of value, even if that value is often overshadowed by the consequences of the passions. It exists and cannot be ignored. It is interesting that the authentic characters are nearly always those who refuse, who say no. (Iphigénie may be the exception in that she obeys her father and accepts the need for the sacrifice.) Despite the element of moral ambiguity that surrounds Monime, she emerges as resolute in her moral opposition to Mithridate. Bajazet eventually refuses to compromise his moral sense any further and reveals the truth about his feelings towards Roxane. Indeed his awareness of perjury emerges in his first scene with Atalide in Act II, scene 5. Aricie refuses to divulge to Thésée what Hippolyte has forbidden her to. The outstanding example in the profane plays is perhaps Junie who cannot bring herself to be false, even when she is ordered to be so by the emperor. All these considerations make the case of Andromaque in Act III, scene 6 even more problematic. Is this her authentic voice? Or is it a voice which imposes a false mode of being, especially in the light of what she recounts of Pyrrhus's exploits in Act III, scene 8? One other element of ambiguity must also be the situation in *Mithridate* where Monime is awaiting the outcome of her disastrous interview with the king in Act IV, scene 1. Phoedime tries to reassure her, saying of Mithridate:

> Ah! traitez-le, Madame, avec plus de justice:
> Un grand roi descend-il jusqu'à cet artifice?

Phoedime at least seems to have in mind that within the voice of a king there should be some sort of moral imperative. This may of course simply be the naiveté of the *confidente.* It nonetheless raises interesting questions about the more general notion of standards of behaviour in Racinian tragedy at the level of voice itself.

One must, however, mention one other character who represents the ultimate in authenticity, Joad. How could this be otherwise for a man who speaks with the voice of his God? But an interpretation of Joad in this light is not without problems, problems similar in fact to those we have encountered with Monime. After all, while Joad does not lie about the treasure that is hidden in the temple, he allows enough ambiguity in the message that Abner will convey to the queen for her to believe that the treasure is of a material sort. The element of ambiguity is compounded rather than lessened by the fact that Joad does not himself speak in such terms to Athalie. That responsibility is carried by one whose own voice has contained an element of ambiguity in the course of the action of the play, Abner's, so that the message itself is not suspect to the queen who is aware of Abner's dual allegiance.

The criterion of authenticity of voice in the tragedies can be further explored through the relation of 'bouche' to 'cœur'. This is sometimes expressed explicitly, using both words, but the relationship is implicit where equivalent words are used. What is at issue here is the degree to which what is enunciated ('bouche') is not the sort of false mode of being we have encountered earlier. The two terms coincide in a voice which excludes all others, where there is a complete coincidence of voice and feeling so absent or so problematic in many Racinian relationships. It is not surprising to find the model of this coincidence contained in the character of Junie:

> Cette sincérité sans doute est peu discrète;
> Mais toujours de mon cœur ma bouche est l'interprète.
> (ll. 639–40)

In other words Junie is incapable of another mode of being through speech. It is no more surprising to find this exact coupling in the religious context of *Esther*, when Esther herself says:

> Que ma bouche et mon cœur, et tout ce que je suis,
> Rendent honneur au Dieu qui m'a donné la vie. (ll. 771–72)

It may happen that such a coincidence is desired by another character, although in Roxane's case it is not so much desired as demanded:

> Je veux que devant moi sa bouche et son visage
> Me découvrent son cœur sans me laisser d'ombrage. (ll. 329–30)

Atalide expresses her concern in a slightly different form when she fears that Bajazet really has declared his love to Roxane:

> Ah, peut-être, après tout, que sans trop se forcer,
> Tout ce qu'il a pu dire, il a pu le penser. (ll. 915–16)

The demand made of others is found in a kinder form in *Bérénice* where Titus has requested of Phoenix that he be the voice of Rome (if Rome is a character in the play, it is in this sense that it is so). In Act II, scene 2 Titus asks Phoenix to fulfil this request: 'Je veux par votre bouche entendre tous les cœurs' (l. 358). Paulin himself, however, is the most representative of those 'cœurs'.

The relationship 'bouche-cœur' is not without its problems. It again falls to Junie to provide the general rule, and thereby give expression to her own exceptional status as a character:

> Je ne connais Néron et la cour que d'un jour,
> Mais, si j'ose le dire, hélas! dans cette cour
> Combien tout ce qu'on dit est loin de ce qu'on pense!
> Que la bouche et le cœur sont peu d'intelligence!
> (ll. 1511–14)

This dislocation of 'bouche' and 'cœur' is evident on many occasions in Racinian tragedy, not least in *Bajazet* where it forms the whole basis of the action. Replying in almost the same terms used earlier by Atalide, Bajazet corrects her impression that he has been able to declare his love to Roxane:

Ah! croyez-vous que, loin de le penser,
Ma bouche seulement eût pu le prononcer? (ll. 979–80)

In *Andromaque*, Oreste discerns that Hermione's 'vœux' are for him but that her 'cœur' is for Pyrrhus (l. 538). This contrasts with what she says about her encounters with Pyrrhus where, as she informs Cléone: 'Je n'ai pour lui parler consulté que mon cœur' (l. 460). Hermione's statement in Act V, scene 3 is much more complex in its implications:

Ah! fallait-il en croire une amante insensée?
Ne devais-tu pas lire au fond de ma pensée?
Et ne voyais-tu pas, dans mes emportements,
Que mon cœur démentait ma bouche à tous moments?
(ll. 1545–48)

Clearly, Hermione did not expect her voice to be taken at its face value.[8] How was Oreste to know this? By what mechanism, a question that Monime might well ask herself, can one judge sincerity? How can one be sure that coincidence of voice and feeling is real? Hermione is ironically in the same position regarding Pyrrhus:

Et qui ne se serait comme moi déclarée
Sur la foi d'une amour si saintement jurée? (ll. 461–62)

This question further confirms that Racinian dialogue is fraught with danger for the characters for they must decide quickly whether they are to believe their interlocutors as they speak.

The dislocation of 'bouche/cœur' is more marked when previously there has been a perfect coincidence between voice and feeling. Such is the case in *Bérénice*. The expectation that the two terms form a whole is well expressed by Bérénice: 'Ce cœur, après huit jours, n'a-t-il rien à me dire?' (l. 580) Indeed part of the reason for Titus choosing a substitute is that he does not wish this dislocation to be evident in his own voice: 'Epargnez à mon cœur cet éclaircissement' (l. 742). As a last resort, when he has finally to confront Bérénice in person, he attempts to remind her of her responsibility for making a potential emperor of him:

Rappelez bien plutôt ce cœur qui tant de fois
M'a fait de mon devoir reconnaître la voix. (ll. 1049–50)

The coupling of 'bouche/cœur' is of course divided here between two characters, but what Titus is trying to suggest to Bérénice is that, at that time, they spoke as one. But then the voice of the emperor was not required since his father was living. His voice was still the voice of love. He has now recognised that this can no longer be so. It is precisely that voice which Bérénice wishes him to maintain. Now, however, he wants Bérénice to endorse his decision to leave her, to adopt, in other words, his voice. Before we leave *Bérénice* we must note another dislocation of 'bouche/cœur' where voice and feeling had been perceived as in harmony. Bérénice refers to Antiochus as 'un ami qui me parle du cœur' (l. 138). We know both that this has been untrue since Antiochus has covered his relations with Titus and Bérénice with 'un voile d'amitié' (l. 26) and that she is about to be disabused. Antiochus substitutes the inauthentic voice of the friend (wherein the dislocation of 'bouche' and 'cœur' is to be located) for one where there will be a real coincidence of voice and feeling when he declares his love for Bérénice.

The relationship of 'bouche' to 'cœur' is of particular note in *Phèdre*. As far as Hippolyte is concerned, he tries in vain to maintain the relationship of these two elements contained in his previous voice, that of the hunter. As he remarks to Théramène:

> Des sentiments d'un cœur si fier, si dédaigneux,
> Peux–tu me demander le désaveu honteux? (ll. 67–68)

Hippolyte has, however, already substituted for his former voice that of the lover, which he fully realises only in his interview with Aricie in the next act.

Implicit in much of what I have written on voice is the possibility of characters possessing or being confronted by a choice, according to the different situations in which they find themselves, situations in which one voice may be preferable to another. Many characters are highly aware of the need to choose, or made aware of this need by others. Œnone impresses on Phèdre the necessity of approaching Hippolyte and of adopting the voice of the mother (ll. 340–48). Monime too knows that her situation requires a particular manner of speaking:

> Peut-être je devrais, plus humble en ma misère,
> Me souvenir du moins que je parle à son frère. (ll. 151–52)

In her turn, she urges Xipharès to abandon the voice of lover for another (ll. 721–26).

At all times, however, the choice is a difficult one, and the tension of utterance reasserts itself. On occasions there is hesitancy. Bajazet has no idea which voice to choose once Atalide has decided to withdraw her assistance: 'Eh bien! Mais quels discours faut-il que je lui tienne?' (l. 786) On the occasion when Bajazet is left alone with Roxane unaided for the first time, in Act II, scene 1, he takes refuge in a sort of 'non-voice'. He has quite simply never been asked, as it were, to use his own. Phèdre too hesitates. She has been beset with the choice between remaining hidden or appearance: this choice of course determines the eventual revelation of her love for her step-son. The hesitancy in Phèdre's choice is evident in Œnone's reaction: 'Comme on voit tous ses vœux l'un l'autre se détruire' (l. 162). A similar fate befalls Athalie, as Nabal remarks to Mathan: 'Qui fait changer ainsi ses vœux irrésolus?' (l. 869). Mathan later uses almost the same words as Œnone to describe the queen: 'Tous ses projets semblaient l'un l'autre se détruire' (l. 887). Mathan himself suspects that Athalie is experiencing a resurgence of maternal feelings (ll. 881–86). Athalie is tempted once again by the voice of the mother, as she will later become mesmerised by the voice of the child.

Néron too faces a difficulty which comes to a head in Act IV. First Burrhus attempts to persuade him to adopt the voice of conciliation and even quotes directly an example of Néron's voice at a time when the emperor took pleasure in his popularity (ll. 1350–54). Through Burrhus Néron hears a model of one possible choice. In the very next scene Narcisse provokes Néron into adopting the voice he has already begun to learn, that of the tyrant.

What is evident here is that the two different voices which constitute choice are often if not always mutually incompatible.[9] Two modes of being cannot coexist: one must be displaced. Xipharès experiences this dilemma in a way when his father, in Act III, scene 1, reveals to the two sons his fantastic plan for marching on Rome. As a warrior himself he supports his father, but which voice can he use now, that of the son or that of the lover? This is why it is strategic for him to address himself first to his brother with whom he is not only a rival in love but also a genuine political opponent. The difficulty arises when he addresses his father, the voice of the lover almost encroaching upon that of the son (ll. 939–40).

The example of Titus is particularly poignant. It has become apparent to him that the voice of the emperor and the voice of the lover are now incompatible. They are even represented by two different directions in terms of space. Paulin urges him:

> Venez, Seigneur, passons dans la chambre prochaine,
> Allons voir le sénat. (ll. 1247–48)

Antiochus encourages him in a different way: 'Ah! courez chez la reine' (l. 1248). In Act V, scene 6 Titus finally concedes that the voice of the lover is now impossible:

> L'empire incompatible avec votre hyménée,
> Me dit qu'après l'éclat et les pas que j'ai faits,
> Je dois vous épouser encor moins que jamais.
> Oui, Madame; et je dois moins encore vous dire
> Que je suis prêt pour vous d'abandonner l'empire. (ll. 1396–97)

A particularly interesting case is constituted by Abner who is in a sense, as we have seen in another context, a classic example of the bureaucrat caught between two allegiances, something of which Athalie is aware:

> Je sais que dès l'enfance élevé dans les armes,
> Abner a le cœur noble, et qu'il rend à la fois
> Ce qu'il doit à son Dieu, ce qu'il doit à ses rois. (ll. 456–57)

The problem for Abner is whether these two voices can act simultaneously. Indeed, Abner attempts to speak as Jew and royal adviser in lines 439–50, but the difficulty he has in doing so is shown by his opening remark: 'Madame, pardonnez si j'ose le défendre' (439). Abner finds a less apologetic voice when he reproaches Mathan for adopting a language inappropriate to his calling as a priest. Mathan is after all a renegade, where at least Athalie has remained loyal to her own god. Unwittingly, Abner also finds himself defending the life of his true king, and Racine underlines this by making Abner conscious of adopting a voice which he would not normally recognise as his:

> Moi, nourri dans la guerre aux horreurs du carnage,
> Des vengeances des rois ministre rigoureux,
> C'est moi qui prête ici ma voix au malheureux! (ll. 572–74)

For Joad who, in religious terms, is the voice of absolute authenticity and univocity, there can be no possibility of choice. He makes this abundantly clear to Abner in Act I, scene 1. He reminds Abner of his previous protestations of fidelity to his God and then informs him of what God would say to him:

> Du zèle de ma loi que sert de vous parer?
> Par de stériles vœux pensez-vous m'honorer?' (ll. 85–86)

There is no such thing as a voice of compromise. Abner must say one thing or the other. He must be a Jew or not.

There are some characters, on the other hand, who discover that they have little or no choice. How can Monime speak to Mithridate in the voice he expects to hear once she has declared her love for Xipharès? Having adopted the voice of love seems to cancel the possibility of any other. Similarly Phèdre finds it difficult to find the voice of the wife and Hippolyte the voice of the son when they come to meet the recently returned Thésée whom they flee at the first opportunity. They are different people by virtue of what has been spoken. The difficulties faced by characters in the matter of choosing a voice can be illustrated at length by the case of Agamemnon in *Iphigénie*. Agamemnon is first presented to us as using the voice of the king:

> Oui, c'est Agamemnon, c'est ton roi qui t'éveille:
> Viens, reconnais la voix qui frappe ton oreille. (ll. 1–2)

He is after all speaking to Arcas and we would not expect any other. But we are soon made to realise that all is not well on the level of voice. Arcas himself detects an undercurrent of unease in the way his master speaks to him: 'Et depuis quand, Seigneur, tenez-vous ce langage?' (l. 13) You are, he adds, covered in honours. The following combination of titles is, however, significant for what is to follow in terms of the choice of voices Agamemnon must subsequently make:

> Roi, père, époux heureux, fils du puissant Atrée,
> Vous possédez des Grecs la plus riche contrée. (ll. 17–18)

It is precisely as neither of these categories that he will be able to speak consistently in the play.

The problem is that Agamemnon has been forced to adopt another voice, that of the order contained in the oracle as it has been revealed and interpreted by Calchas: 'Sacrifiez Iphigénie' (l. 62). This is the voice that Agamemnon does his best to avoid. Agamemnon even suggests that if he does not speak as the king, he will be deprived of his power, as indeed eventually happens (ll. 134–41). It is however in a sense more complex than this, since Ulysse reminds the king that it was he who had called them all to war:

> N'est-ce pas vous enfin de qui la voix pressante
> Nous a tous appelés aux campagnes du Xanthe. (ll. 297–98)

Using the voice of a king means that you must be a king. But the voice of the king is a reluctant one:

> Je me rendis, Arcas; et vaincu par Ulysse,
> De ma fille, en pleurant, j'ordonnai le supplice. (ll. 89–90)

It is indeed with Ulysse that one might expect Agamemnon to use the voice of the king, but it is precisely with Ulysse that we hear the voice of the king waver in a scene of public importance, because the third interlocutor is Achille. It is significant, moreover, that this should occur in Act I, scene 2, as if to illustrate what the king has himself explained to Arcas. One reason for Agamemnon's equivocation is his fear that Achille will have discovered the stratagem he has used to lure his wife and daughter to Aulis. Ulysse has to reply for Agamemnon who has been taken aback by Achille's arrival. Another reason is the militancy with which Achille wishes to pursue the task of moving on to Troy. Agamemnon knows that the departure of the army will coincide with his order to sacrifice Iphigénie, all of which reminds him of the consequences of using the voice of the king.

In *Iphigénie* the voice of the father in fact conflicts with that of the king. They are incompatible and not interchangeable. One must yield to the other. It is interesting that in the first instance the voice of the father is in written form in the letter Arcas must take to Iphigénie and her mother in order to prevent them from arriving. He fails in this endeavour and must confront his daughter in Act II, scene 2 where he finds it impossible to speak in the voice of the father. This is clearly discerned by Iphigénie herself:

> Hé! mon père, oubliez votre rang à ma vue,
> Je prévois la rigueur d'un long éloignement.
> N'osez-vous sans rougir être père un moment. (ll. 558–60)

Agamemnon in this instance hides behind the voice of the king. A similar situation obtains in Act III, scene 1 where Agamemnon again adopts the voice of the king, this time with his wife:

> Vous avez entendu ce que je vous demande,
> Madame, je le veux, et je vous le commande.
> Obéissez. (ll. 818–19)

Agamemnon is in a very significant way the 'inauthentic' husband since he is concealing the truth from his wife about their daughter's future. Clytemnestre expects perhaps, in the matter of their daughter's marriage, for the voice of the king and the father/husband to coincide. When the queen finally learns the truth, she challenges her husband at the very root of his power, that is to say, his voice as a king, the voice which has called them to war, the voice which will order the sacrifice (l. 1261 sq. and l. 1283sq.). The remarkable aspect of the whole process is the role of Iphigénie herself in this scene. In accepting the sacrifice, she substitutes her own voice for that of Agamemnon. She takes on, through her obedience, the voice of the king and, in her love for Agamemnon, the voice of the father:

> Mon père,
> Cessez de vous troubler, vous n'êtes point trahi.
> Quand vous commanderez, vous serez obéi.
> Ma vie est votre bien; vous voulez le reprendre:
> Vos ordres sans détour pouvaient se faire entendre.
> D'un œil aussi content, d'un cœur aussi soumis
> Que j'acceptais l'époux que vous m'aviez promis,
> Je saurai, s'il le faut, victime obéissante,
> Tendre au fer de Calchas une tête innocente,
> Et respectant le coup par vous-même ordonné,
> Vous rendre tout le sang que vous m'avez donné. (ll. 1170–80)

She addresses both the father and the king, and in so doing, releases Agamemnon from the responsibility of having to choose between the voice of the father and the king, which he cannot, in addressing her. It is somewhat ironic therefore that the play, apart from the last two lines of Clytemnestre, should end with the voice of a king reestablished through the intermediary of Ulysse. Agamemnon is no longer able to speak for himself at all.

Voice substitution at all levels is thus problematic and plays its part in the tragic experience. It is an act of speech, and in some cases of non-speech, which is bound to have consequences for others. Voice substitution can, for example, be a way of denying the other, or at least that is how it is perceived. Titus thinks he can send Bérénice away simply by not speaking to her. In addition, usurping the voice of another character is inevitably acting upon that character in a negative way, taking away what has been theirs. In that sense, voice substitution is a deliberate appropriation, or seen from another point of view, deprivation. But substitution within a character has similar effects. Néron acts upon Junie by adopting the new voice gained through the discourse of love, and deprives his mother of a voice that was formerly shared with him. Titus, by adopting the voice of emperor, deprives himself and Bérénice of the voice of love.

What is significant is that almost all forms of voice substitution fail. Néron loses Junie and Atalide is deprived of Bajazet. Arcas misses Iphigénie and Clytemnestre. Oreste signally fails as Hermione's messenger. The need to confront others remains. Speaking for oneself, and as oneself, whatever self is represented by speech at a given moment, can never be avoided. Characters cannot hide behind quotation. The imperative of the visual and the vocal remains at the heart of the Racinian tragic experience.

Chapter 4
Speech and Time

The concept of Racinian tragedy that I have sought to promote in this study rests in part on the premiss that the drama in the plays is constituted by a transaction to be negotiated until such time that it reaches a conclusion. The characters must enunciate a decision which will bring an end to the transaction, although for a variety of reasons the final decision is difficult or impossible to pronounce. In this context time is made up of speech moments, each of which is crucial to the outcome of the action. Time can therefore be measured in terms of presence, since the characters' future depends on performing the right sort of language at the right moment. The way acts of speech relate to time in the past, present and future is the subject of this chapter.

In the first place, of course, Racine invests the issue to which all speech is directed with considerable urgency. Characters have to reply or to enunciate certain things within a defined period. They are issued with an ultimatum. For example, Roxane insists that, if Bajazet loves her: 'dès ce jour il me doit épouser' (l. 288). As we have seen in Chapter 2 he must himself speak alone in her presence: 'Sa perte ou son salut dépend de sa réponse' (l. 326). Once the negotiation of the transaction has begun it has a clearly defined time limit. The terminus of this period is even more clearly marked when Bajazet is asked by Roxane: 'Pour la dernière fois, veux-tu vivre et régner?' (l. 1541) In *Andromaque* Pyrrhus makes it perfectly clear to Hector's widow in Act III that she has one last chance to decide whether to save her son or not by agreeing to marriage. Titus knows that he cannot prolong his dismissal of Bérénice. Joad is told in *Athalie*: 'La reine impatiente attend votre réponse' (l. 983). The ultimatum is always a question of speech, a matter of saying something. The ultimatum is not about marriage, let us say, it is about agreeing to marriage.

In these circumstances Racinian characters cannot entertain leisure in speech. Bajazet warns Atalide: 'Et ne prolongez point de dangereux adieux' (l. 676). Similarly Monime urges on Xipharès that indulgence in speech is perilous (ll. 739–42). Abner exhorts Joad not to delay his reply to the queen:

> Le temps est cher, Seigneur, plus que vous ne pensez.
> Tandis qu'à me répondre ici vous balancez,

> Mathan près d'Athalie étincelant de rage,
> Demande le signal et presse le carnage. (ll. 1629–32)

Characters even perceive speech as in itself time-wasting. This may be limited to certain categories of speech which are not relevant to the specific transaction of the play. Acomat is not prepared to spend precious moments in explaining to Osmin how it is that they are now conversing in the previously forbidden harem. This is regarded as 'discours superflus' (l. 8). In the same way Xipharès does not, in the first scene of *Mithridate*, consider it the time to 'rappeler le cours d'une amoureuse histoire' (l. 42). Mithridate's return concentrates Pharnace's mind to the extent that he is willing to consign a discussion of rivalry in love to another time (l. 341).

One might imagine then that the present tense is everything in Racine. But the present speech of the characters is related to other times in rather specific ways. Speech in the plays, for example, has a past, and it is often in the light of past speech that present speech attains a specific level of significance. Other times may imply other conditions of speech. What is crucial therefore is the change in speech conditions which operates between the past and present of the action we see and hear. We shall once again be confronted with the discontinuity rather than continuity of voice I referred to in the previous chapter.

One form of continuity might however derive from past speech being used to legitimate speech in the present. Atalide informs us that Bajazet and she have loved each other from childhood but had been separated on the death of his mother (ll. 357–365). This is later confirmed by Bajazet to Roxane (ll. 1496–97). From that moment: 'nous avons su toujours nous aimer et nous taire' (l. 366). While certainly the love of Atalide and Bajazet is a measure against which we view Roxane's passion for the brother of Amurat, the conditions of its enunciation have changed so dramatically that the dialogue between them cannot be considered continuous since it is now directed at another character, Roxane. It is a different situation completely.

The love of Monime and Xipharès too is legitimised by the fact that it predates that of the king for Monime. Xipharès reminds Arbate that he had met Monime before Mithridate had even heard of her (ll. 45–48) and impresses upon Monime herself the anteriority, and therefore the legitimacy, of his love for her (ll. 191–96). In their case however there is no continuity of dialogue as such since they had not spoken of their love for each other before the action of the play begins. The continuity of their dialogue is thus a matter for the future rather than possessing a relationship to the past.

A similar situation in fact occurs in Bérénice. Antiochus has only the feelings of love to legitimate his discourse of love with Bérénice since it was his brother who spoke for him in the first instance. Any communication of his own with the Palestinian queen became impermissible after she had met Titus (ll. 189–98). It is clear that some communication took place because:

> Je disputai longtemps, je fis parler mes yeux;
> Mes pleurs et mes soupirs vous suivaient en tous lieux. (ll. 201–2)

In this sense his confession to Bérénice is a new departure in terms of the sort of speech it entails (he has been a confidant of the queen) and one which is destined to have no future. As a final comment on this aspect of speech, it is interesting that it should be Hermione who reminds Oreste that he was the first to stir in her the flame of love (ll. 533–34).

So, in the past a general context of speech exists which contributes directly to the situation of speech in the present. But the case of Antiochus makes us ask what sort of record of speech there is between the characters. Speech from the past may simply be described as a *récit*. Iphigénie, for example, tells her father how she enjoyed being told of his future conquests (ll. 1195–96). Hippolyte took pleasure in hearing of the heroic exploits of his father (ll. 73–82), but put an end to the account of his less glorious affairs (ll. 83–92). The *récit* helps to situate in some way past to present speech, in these two cases, by Iphigénie justifying her own sacrifice (the future conquest being that of Troy), and by Hippolyte wishing that he could be the subject of heroic discourse (in slaying monsters like his father).

But the most frequent category of recorded speech from the past concerns the discourse of love. It may be recounted in general terms, such as the 'cent messages secrets' which have passed between Cléophile and Alexandre. Or it may be more detailed in the way that Titus and Bérénice have seen and talked with each other daily for five years. Sometimes, however, speech in the past has only ever been in potential. It could have been articulated but wasn't. Such is the case with Monime and Xipharès. Phoedime mentions that Monime has been troubled in the past by her love for Xipharès (ll. 395–96). Indeed exchange would have been possible at that stage, since Monime remarks:

> Et je ne savais pas que, pour moi plein de feux,
> Xipharès des mortels fût le plus amoureux. (ll. 401–2)

The action of the play actualises the potential of the past. This is further reflected in Xipharès's observation to Monime that she must have been aware of his plaintive voice at the time of their earlier separation (ll. 199–202). It should be noted that Racine takes particular care to note the quality of voice in past situations.

A precise function is therefore ascribed to the record of past speech in the present. Andromaque offers her persuasive powers over Hector in the past as a model of behaviour for Hermione whom she begs to intercede on Andromaque's behalf with Pyrrhus:

> Hélas! lorsque, lassés de dix ans de misère,
> Les Troyens en courroux menaçaient votre mère,
> J'ai su de mon Hector lui procurer l'appui. (ll. 873–75)

Perhaps the most crucial aspect of speech in the past which operates in the present is that of oaths and promises, truly 'performative' acts, which are important in that they represent a commitment made in the past which must be now fulfilled. In a sense promises or oaths are not 'past' speech at all. They constitute an eternally present commitment. The vital element of commitment in the promise or oath is that it sets up an expectation in the character to whom the promise is made. Present speech is always regarded as a renewal of the promise in the way it will commit a character to the fulfilment of that promise. Axiane expects that Alexandre will not regard those he has conquered as enemies (ll. 1375–76). Equally Alexandre had promised Cléophile that his conquests would eventually mean that he would return to her (ll. 855–56). In *La Thébaïde* the two brothers had sworn to respect the order that each would in turn be king of Thebes (l. 87). Achille is determined that he will get what was promised to him: 'On ne m'abuse point par des promesses vaines' (l. 1349).

The implication of the promise and the oath is that the value of that promise or oath very much depends on the person who makes it. There are thus promises which are above suspicion. Axiane is in love with Porus and swears to him 'une amitié si longtemps attendue' (l. 993). Xipharès, before Monime declares her love for him, promises to respect her independence: 'Vous voulez être à vous, j'en ai donné ma foi' (l. 181). Hippolyte's commitment to offer marriage to Aricie before the gods is also above suspicion (ll. 1399–1406). Such promises offer continuity between past and present, although in certain cases this is never actually fulfilled. Some promises are on the other hand less promising. It is known in advance that they cannot be delivered. They do not ensure the future. When Agrippine tells Britannicus:

> J'ai promis, il suffit. Malgré vos ennemis,
> Je ne révoque rien de ce que j'ai promis (ll. 917–18),

we know that her power is already undermined by Néron's efforts to render her voice ineffective.

Other promises are made reluctantly, which makes their certain delivery all the more poignant. Agamemnon has promised his daughter in sacrifice (ll.285–88), and spends a good deal of the action in attempting to nullify the effect of his promise. For example he attempts to rid himself of Achille by absolving him of his oath to make war on Troy with the other Greeks (ll. 1398–99). None of this prevents Iphigénie from going to the altar of sacrifice. It is divine intervention which 'delivers' the promise in an unexpected way. Or a promise may be delivered all too effectively, as with Neptune's promise to Thésée:

> Souviens-toi que pour prix de mes efforts heureux
> Tu promis d'exaucer le premier de mes vœux. (ll. 1067–68)

Mistakenly Aricie thinks it possible for Hippolyte to reverse the effect of the promise in persuading Thésée of the truth of his situation (ll. 1335–56).

One category of promise which can never be doubted is that of divine promise embodied in Scripture. God's promise to the Jews is recounted by Esther:

> Mon père mille fois m'a dit dans mon enfance
> Qu'avec nous tu juras (=God) une sainte alliance. (ll. 249–50)

It is however precisely this promise which is doubted by Abner:

> Mais où sont ces honneurs à David tant promis,
> Et prédits même encore à Salomon son fils? (ll. 129–30)

The special quality of divine promise is explained by Joad in that the word of God 'est stable et ne trompe jamais' (l. 158). Joad of course is the human instrument whereby that word can be fulfilled, thus linking the voice of the past with the present. But promises in a religious context are not always proof against human fragility. Joad asks Joas whether he will swear always to be faithful (ll. 1381–82) and orders him to swear on the Scriptures. Joas pronounces:

> Je promets d'observer ce que la loi m'ordonne.
> Mon Dieu, punissez-moi si je vous abandonne. (ll. 1409–10)

Joad's own prophecy fortells Joas's failure to honour that promise.

Indeed, Racine's plays are very often plays of broken vows. In this sense discontinuity in speech, as we shall see in a number of specific instances, is more frequent than continuity. Racine began his theatrical career with a subject where reneging on a promise is the centre of dramatic focus and has as its consequences carnage on a grand scale. As Polynice says of Etéocle:

> Je ne veux rien de lui que ce qu'il m'a promis:
> Il ne saurait régner sans se rendre parjure. (ll. 1034–35)

In *Alexandre* Taxile is described by Porus as 'un amant infidèle et parjure' (l. 274) and the same word 'parjure' is used in the case of Agamemnon by Achille (l. 973).

It is interesting, however, to examine oaths and promises in three tragedies where they are particularly central to the structure of the tragedy as a whole, *Andromaque*, *Bérénice* and *Bajazet*. There are several perspectives on broken promises in *Andromaque*. A promise not only marks a commitment on the part of the person who makes the promise. It also commits to a certain action the person to whom the promise is made. Such is the case with Hermione:

> Et qui ne se serait comme moi déclarée
> Sur la foi d'une amour si saintement jurée? (ll. 461–62)

Hermione thus engages upon the discourse of love on the basis of Pyrrhus's oath, the promise being an act of speech which determines one way or another all future patterns of speech. But Pyrrhus is the breaker of promises and a character who constantly goes back on his word. He admits this to Andromaque: 'Je sais de quels serments je romps pour vous la chaîne' (l. 961). In this light Andromaque's evaluation of Pyrrhus in Act IV, scene 1 is a curious one. Céphise is sure that Pyrrhus will not renege on his promise to ensure the safety of her son: 'Pyrrhus vous l'a promis' (l. 1053). Andromaque adds later:

> Je sais quel est Pyrrhus: violent mais sincère,
> Céphise, il fera plus qu'il n'a promis de faire. (ll. 1085–86)

Pyrrhus says to Hermione:

> Oui, Madame, et j'avoue
> Que je vous ai promis la foi que je lui voue. (ll. 1281–82)

This is precisely what Hermione herself throws back at him: 'Va lui jurer la foi que tu m'avais jurée' (l. 1381). Pyrrhus does not expect his feelings to be spared: 'Donnez-moi tous les noms destinés aux parjures' (l. 1305).

But one of the most interesting features of oaths and promises in *Andromaque* is the way in which both Pyrrhus and Hermione attempt to shift the responsibility away from their own personal commitment. Hermione says to Oreste once Pyrrhus has decided — temporarily — to return to her:

> Mais que puis-je, Seigneur, on a promis ma foi.
> Lui ravirai-je un bien qui ne tient pas de moi? (ll. 819–20)

Pyrrhus uses a similar argument when Andromaque urges him to return to the daughter of Helen: 'Je sais que de mes vœux on lui promit l'empire' (l. 345). Pyrrhus repeats this less than committed view of his promise to Hermione in Act IV, scene 5:

> Un autre vous dirait que dans les champs troyens
> Nos deux pères sans nous formèrent ces liens,
> Et que sans consulter ni mon choix ni le vôtre,
> Nous fûmes sans amour engagés l'un à l'autre;
> Mais c'est assez pour moi que je me sois soumis.
> Par mes ambassadeurs mon cœur vous fut promis;
> Loin de les révoquer, je voulus y souscrire. (ll. 1283–89)

Bérénice begins with a broken promise. Antiochus, despite his oath, declares his love for Bérénice to her face. Antiochus breaks a silence he had not only promised but sworn. 'Jurer' is consequently in a higher category than 'promettre'. Past speech in any case has a sharper focus in *Bérénice* than in many other Racinian tragedies because it contains repeated oaths. Bérénice can refer to the 'serments redoublés mille fois' of Titus (l. 173), to 'mille serments appuyés de mes larmes' (l. 440), which makes his words of separation all the more painful: 'Après tant de serments, Titus m'abandonner' (l. 906).

But *Bérénice* is a play of oaths and promises which conflict with each other. It suggests moreover that one form of oath can cancel another. After all Titus has sworn his love for Bérénice ('Titus me jurait [...]' l. 907) but must now swear his allegiance to the Empire:

> Je frémis. Mais enfin, quand j'acceptai l'empire,
> Rome me fit jurer de maintenir ses droits. (ll. 1156–57)

Ironically it is only an oath from Bérénice at the end of the play which will resolve the situation. Following the threats of suicide contained in the letter Titus has torn from Bérénice's hands, he asks:

> Si vous ne me jurez d'en (=vie) respecter le cours,
> Madame, à d'autres pleurs vous devez vous attendre. (ll. 1418–19)

Oaths and promises on a human level, that is to say within individual relationships, can never be eternal, and emphasise discontinuity in speech rather than continuity. The two forms of promise which are regarded as eternal are those made to the state on the one hand and the word of God on the other.[1]

There are a number of promises in *Bajazet*, the strangest of which in one way is the promise giving Atalide to Acomat in which Bajazet himself seems to have played a part (l. 176), although no more is made of this in the course of the play. Bajazet has also been promised the empire (l. 427), as long as he replies to Roxane's demands for love in the way she wishes him to do. The most significant aspect of promises in the play is that Bajazet refuses to perjure himself although this will certainly lead to his death. Acomat urges on the prince the salvation that his promise will bring:

> Promettez. Affranchi d'un péril qui vous presse,
> Vous verrez de quel poids est votre promesse. (ll. 641–42)

Indeed Acomat does not invest the same weight in a promise as Bajazet: 'le sang des Ottomans / Ne doit point en esclave obéir aux serments' (ll. 643–44). At one point Bajazet's refusal to promise love to Roxane seems to rest on the fear that he would be found out (ll. 743–46). But it is clear that he has moral objections too:

> Et j'irais l'abuser d'une fausse promesse?
> Je me parjurerais? (ll. 753–34)

This would especially be the case given that Atalide has been the recipient of his 'serments redoublés' (l. 716). Bajazet can only make to Roxane a promise of a general sort:

> Oui, je vous ai promis et j'ai donné ma foi
> De n'oublier jamais tout ce que je vous doi. (ll. 1027–28)

Bajazet thus refuses to commit himself to a future of dishonesty in speech, since obviously his would be a promise to enunciate feelings he does not experience.

In this discussion of the relation of present to past speech continuity or discontinuity has been an important feature, especially in the way speech conditions may have changed. This would be especially true of those characters who meet each other again after a period of separation. Can they simply pick up where they left off? How does this renewal of dialogue work out?

The conditions of speech in the action of *Mithridate* are entirely distinct from those that had obtained in the past as recorded by the characters. The king is reported to be dead so that Xipharès and Pharnace feel free to express their love for Monime. Previously Xipharès and Monime have spoken together but not of their feelings for each other. In fact the play represents the impossibility of reproducing in the present a form of discourse that has prevailed in the past. Before the action of the play begins, Monime has had no occasion on which to express her love to Xipharès who himself has only implied his love for her. She has adopted therefore, on the occasion of her betrothal to the king, the voice of obedience. In Act I, scene 2 this love has been confirmed to her and it is welcome. When she meets Mithridate on his return she again adopts the voice of obedience but obviously unwillingly, as he himself recognises (ll. 551–52). The fact is that another form of speech, rooted in the immediate present, is now possible. Mithridate reproaches her later in the play for not having informed him earlier that marriage to him was repugnant for her: 'Avant que de partir, pourquoi vous taisiez-vous?' (l. 1302) The reason for this is simply that the voice she is now able to produce, that is to say a voice of refusal and self-assertion, did not exist in the past. In fact his own discourse of power prevented it. Ironically it is in the same speech that Mithridate demands from her the voice of obedience, her past discourse, which she can no longer ressucitate (ll. 1293 sq). There is some ambiguity, however, about what sort of recommencement of dialogue Mithridate expects in Act II, scene 4. Is it of the discourse of love? But we know that even before Xipharès's declaration of love she viewed the prospect of marriage with the king with feelings well short of enthusiasm. So how different is Monime's speech in this scene? What did it contain before that is missing now?

In *Britannicus* Agrippine and Néron recommence their dialogue, but the speech conditions have changed to the extent that the young emperor is now seeking to find a voice of his own. The play in fact *initiates* dialogue between them since Néron's voice has previously been indistinguishable from that of his mother. In the case of Oreste it could be held that the speech conditions with Hermione are more or less the same. He arrives in Epire and discovers that Pyrrhus is unlikely to relinquish Astyanax, hoping therefore that he will be able to leave with Hermione. But he eventually harbours few illusions about the way in which Hermione views dialogue with him. Indeed, in the course of the play he is unable to find new grounds for dialogue, and their relationship continues in the discontinuous way that it has in the past.

As on so many occasions in the course of my analyses, expectation is at the centre of the dramatic focus in the renewal of dialogue. In fact expectation of renewal is itself a constituent element of the tragic situation in *Andromaque*, since Hermione continually hopes that Pyrrhus will return to her. This happens once in the play:

> Qui l'eût cru que Pyrrhus ne fût pas infidèle?
> Que sa flamme attendrait si tard pour éclater?
> Qu'il reviendrait à moi quand je l'allais quitter? (ll. 810–12)

Almost like Oreste, Antiochus knows in advance the reception that he will receive from Bérénice and is indeed dismissed by her. But on two occasions (Act II, scene 2 and Act V, scene 2) he is allowed, albeit with misgivings, to hope that a renewal of dialogue will be possible. Bérénice of course awaits a different outcome from her reunion with Titus after the end of his period of mourning, when he is expected to return 'aux soins de son amour' (l. 57). She is as yet unaware that Titus's decision will prevent a return to their previous conditions of speech.

If renewal of dialogue sets up the expectation that past speech can be repeated, the tragedy lies in the fact that, in many plays, speech must come to an end. The action of the play is a veritable terminus of dialogue. Andromaque's repeated resistance to Pyrrhus's daily attempts to persuade her to marry him and her repeated refusals ensure that Pyrrhus will return to the daughter of Helen, an act that has been repeated on a number of occasions:

> Hermione elle-même a vu plus de cent fois
> Cet amant irrité revenir sous ses lois. (ll. 115–16)

The action of the play in effect offers us a model of past speech as it has progressed.[2] Act I, scene 4 shows us the situation in the exact order in which Pylade has described it to Oreste, the attempted persuasion of Andromaque and the return to Hermione. The difference, of course, is that Oreste's arrival places pressure on the characters to secure a conclusion to their problem. Repetition of past patterns of dialogue in the action of the play itself is also the fate, not to say the perverse desire, of Oreste:

> Ils (= Hermione's eyes) n'ont pour avancer cette mort où je cours
> Qu'à me dire une fois ce qu'ils m'ont dit toujours. (ll. 492–3)

Every time is one last time, the time which would put an end to a dialogue which has been endlessly repeated.

In *Bérénice* the pattern of repetition in dialogue is however a feature rooted in the past conditions of speech which Titus and Bérénice have shared, as Titus himself affirms:

> Je me suis fait un plaisir nécessaire
> De la voir chaque jour, de l'aimer, de lui plaire. (ll. 423–34)

Titus has seen Bérénice every day for the last five years, yet 'croit toujours la voir pour la première fois' (l. 545). Each time he has spoken to her has represented a new beginning to dialogue between them, and it is precisely that renewal that he must now seek to avoid. The strength of the theme of this sort of repetition is embodied in the following outburst of Titus in the final act of the play:

> Connaissez-moi, Madame, et depuis cinq années,
> Comptez tous les moments et toutes les journées
> Où par plus de transports et par plus de soupirs,
> Je vous ai de mon cœur exprimé les désirs. (ll. 1339–42)

The repetition of these words of love has now to come to an end. This is disconcerting for Bérénice because in the past it is reassurance that has come from repetition:

> Mais non, il a cent fois
> Rassuré mon amour contre leurs dures lois. (ll. 641–42)

In fact Titus, by the beginning of the action of the play, has already decided to call a halt to the discourse of love. What is repeated in the play is his failure to enunciate that decision. Ironically the speech that had been banned, that of Antiochus, becomes the instrument which is intended to redress that failure and is repeated at crucial moments in the course of the action.

That an end to dialogue or to speech contributes to the tragic impact in Racinian drama can be illustrated further by reference to many other tragedies. Néron orders Junie to end all communication with Britannicus (ll. 673–74). This is all the more difficult because: 'Ma bouche mille fois lui jura le contraire' (l. 676). But an end to dialogue may be signalled in in the most brutal way, such as the dismissal of Bajazet by Roxane. She says simply: 'Je ne vous dis plus rien' (ll. 1490). Ironically, in *Mithridate*, the end of dialogue coincides (or so Monime intends and leads Xipharès to think at the time) with its beginning. Monime declares her love to the prince but insists on obeying Mithridate, thus terminating her communication with Xipharès (ll. 696–98).

One particular phrase of Racine underlines the finality of an end to speech or dialogue. Atalide, who must abandon Bajazet to his own devices, remarks:

> Je ne vous voyais pas ainsi que je vous vois,
> Prêt à me dire adieu *pour la dernière fois.* (ll. 691–92)

Roxane can tolerate the situation of doubt no further and will consult Bajazet 'pour la dernière fois' (l. 257). A similar finality is imparted to Titus's intention to see Bérénice: 'Et je vais lui parler pour la dernière fois' (l. 490). The phrase is repeated by Junie in the scene before Britannicus unwittingly goes to his death: 'Et si je vous parlais pour la dernière fois' (l. 1536). It is interesting that a phrase so celebrated in Racinian tragedy for marking finality should in so many cases be associated with speech. This finality is all the more painful in that it dashes all hopes of the future dialogue that has been expected and desired by the characters. Titus complains:

> Mes transports aujourd'hui s'attendaient d'éclater;
> Cependant aujourd'hui, Prince, il faut la quitter. (ll. 713–14)

Moreover the end of dialogue is seen as death, as Bérénice implies (ll. 615–16). Speech is life.

On some occasions the characters have each time to relive finality. In *Bajazet* the end to speech can come at any moment. Every confrontation between Bajazet and Roxane could be the last. As she herself says: 'S'il m'échappait un mot, c'est fait de votre vie' (l. 542). In *Andromaque* an end to dialogue (through departure) is constantly threatened by Hermione: 'Toujours prête à partir et demeurant toujours' (l. 131). How many more times will Pyrrhus repudiate Hermione or abandon Andromaque? Each reversal is an end to one pattern of dialogue. As Pylade remarks to Oreste:

> Pensez-vous, quand Pyrrhus vous l'aurait accordée,
> Qu'un prétexte tout prêt ne l'eût pas retardée? (ll. 749–50)

Pyrrhus then exhibits all the features of *false finality*. He claims that he has abandoned the discourse of love with Andromaque (l. 633sq), and confidently announces: 'D'un amour qui s'éteint c'est le dernier éclat' (l. 704). Given the weakness of Pyrrhus in his dealing with the two women it is therefore surprising that he meets Hermione in Act IV, scene 5 in order to tell her that his relationship with her is at an end. It is almost as if the end is not an end unless it is spoken. Perhaps this is why Hermione desires that Pyrrhus should know at the wedding ceremony that he is being killed on account of her.

There are other examples of false finality in the tragedies. Abner (wrongly) claims that God is silent: 'L'arche sainte est muette, et ne rend plus d'oracles' (l. 103), whereas, in *Esther*, the massacre of the Jews would put an end to their voice. It is the daughters of Zion who maintain the record of the people:

> Non, non, ne souffre pas que ces peuples farouches,
> Ivres de notre sang, ferment les seules bouches
> Qui dans tout l'univers célèbrent tes bienfaits. (ll. 269–71)

In fact the order will be revoked, thus ensuring the survival of the Jews.

Silence plays its part — one would not expect otherwise in Racine — in this concept of false finality. Monime must silence the voice of love in order to return to that of obedience. In the event she is permitted to return to the discourse of love she shares with Xipharès. Antiochus thinks that he has returned to the silence imposed on him by Bérénice where he relinquished the discourse of lover for that of the friend and companion. He bids an 'éternel adieu' to Bérénice. But 'éternel' can also signify 'endless'. Antiochus will see Bérénice on two more occasions in the play. It is therefore with a certain irony that we hear him say to Titus: 'La reine pour jamais a reçu mes adieux' (l. 702).

The end to dialogue is sometimes, of course, a function of power. But that power is frequently illusory. It is Andromaque's decision, and not that of Pyrrhus which controls the direction of speech in the play. Although it may appear that Roxane controls the end of dialogue in *Bajazet*, that control is in effect false: an order has already left the battlefield which renders the whole action of the play redundant. The illusion of control of dialogue is illustrated in stark form in *Britannicus*. Agrippine thinks she has lost it:

> Non, non, le temps n'est plus que Néron, jeune encore,
> Me renvoyait les vœux d'une cour qui l'adore,
> Lorsqu'il se reposait sur moi de tout l'Etat,
> Que mon ordre au palais assemblait le sénat. (ll. 91–94)

She constantly reassures Britannicus, on the other hand, that her power is intact and indeed believes herself to have regained power over her son. We come to know that her promises to the young couple cannot be delivered. Equally Néron, who believes that at last he has found his own voice with which to exercise power, is ultimately the victim of an illusion. Junie's departure puts an end to the dialogue that was to replace the discourse his mother controlled. It is not so much power over lives that is at the forefront of Racinian tragedy. It is power over their speech. But that power does not ensure control, as Mithridate too discovers in his relationship with Monime.

So far I have considered speech which moves in some way from the past into the present. Not all conditions of speech, however, fall into this category. Conditions of speech can be created in the course of the action itself. Characters, as I have had occasion to note, discover a new voice. In this case therefore we witness the initiation rather than the renewal of dialogue. Indeed we can identify sets of characters who meet in the action of plays for the very first time. This in itself may possess highly dramatic qualities as with the encounter in Act II, scene 7 of Athalie with Joas, the boy she had prophetically seen in a dream the night before. The same is true of Néron and Junie, especially since Racine emphasises that Junie had previously shunned the dazzle of the court (ll. 415–17). Nor is there a record of speech between Hippolyte and Aricie before the action of the play begins. Indeed he speaks to her a form of language he has never previously spoken. Hence, as spectators, we share with Aricie the experience of language at its origins. Although Hippolyte and Phèdre have obviously met (her first encounter with him is graphically described in lines 269–97), Racine takes care to foreground in Phèdre's description of this past meeting sight rather than speech, thus imparting a particular dramatic effect to their first meeting in the play. Each character is using an unfamiliar language which inevitably increases the tension of utterance. In *Bajazet* the initiation of dialogue coincides with the 'opening' of the harem, the significance of which I discussed in my second chapter.

The creation of new speech conditions and new voices is sometimes marked by an end to silence. Acomat urges Roxane: 'Déclarons-nous, Madame, et rompons le silence' (l. 225). Hippolyte is conscious of this new beginning through intitiating speech:

> Puisque j'ai commencé de rompre le silence,
> Madame, il faut poursuivre. (ll. 526–27)

That Hippolyte's voice of love has never been heard before is proved tragically by his horses who no longer recognise him (l. 552 and l. 1536). In one way of course Aricie herself is released from silence since she has previously been debarred from having interlocutors, at least in the significant area of love.

New speech conditions can also be identified however when characters hear things for the first time and it is in this way that it is possible to interpret the celebrated embarrassment of Hippolyte with Phèdre in Act II, scene 5 (Aricie does not declare her love for Hippolyte but hints at it towards the end of Act II, scene 2). Indeed Phèdre offers this as an explanation herself, although she misinterprets the situation as a whole. Interestingly enough the innocence of Hippolyte's discourse is precisely what Aricie demands:

> Pour moi, je suis plus fière et fuis la gloire aisée
> D'arracher un hommage à mille autres offert. (ll. 445–56)

He would not speak to her as he would have spoken to others. It would be virgin speech as well as the speech of a virgin.

So, speech in the past, as it is recounted by the characters, has a direct relation to speech in the present, to speech as enunciated in the course of the play itself. Let us pass now to speech in the present because speech in time, the performance of speech, determines in some way the 'being' of the characters. As I have noted, speech is life. The 'being' of the characters consists of those moments of speech which, counted as they are, are necessary for 'talking out' the problem, the issue, or the transaction which, in a limited space of time, needs to be brought to a conclusion in an exchange with another character. Stage time, their appearance before others, represents the being of characters. They depend for their existence on speech.[3] This is what I call 'speech time'. Speech time can exist on a personal level but it is only really effective when it is part of an exchange with another major character. It is more effective still when characters share a speech time based on the convergence of speech I discussed in the first chapter.

The degree to which speech and being are one is most poignantly illustrated by Bérénice. Bérénice's existence is defined by seeking opportunities to speak to Titus:

> Elle passe ses jours, Paulin, sans rien prétendre
> Que quelque heure à me voir, et le reste à m'attendre. (ll. 535–36)

That speech with Titus occupies her whole life is parallelled by Titus occupying the whole of her speech. Antiochus gives Bérénice the following reason for leaving Rome:

> Je fuis Titus: je fuis ce nom qui m'inquiète,
> Ce nom qu'à tous moments votre bouche répète. (ll. 274–75)

Characters exist in time through speech by means of which they achieve their highest degree of being, even — and this is the essence of Racinian tragedy — if that speech causes suffering. As we shall see, love in particular is a feeling which, without speech, does not engage the 'being' of the characters.

The main essence of speech however is that it punctuates time. Effectively, Racinian tragedy generally demonstrates a movement, whose vehicle is speech, from non-time to time. The concept of undifferentiated time is particularly important in the domain of love. For Phèdre the beginnings of her love are not associated with speech: 'Mes yeux ne voyaient plus, je ne pouvais parler' (l. 275). Her downfall dates precisely from the moment she speaks to Hippolyte, from the moment she enters speech time in an exchange which projects the enunciation of her love further than the private encounter with Œnone. Phèdre has sought a non-time in another sort of language, that is to say a language directed away from her love: 'Par des vœux assidus je crus les (= tourments inévitables) détourner' (l. 279). Phèdre bans language directed to her love by prohibiting the mention of Hippolyte's name (ll. 603–4). This situation could have continued indefinitely, especially since Hippolyte's absence avoided any possibility of speech with him. It is with Thésée's death, and her need to intercede for her son that she enters the speech time she so wished to avoid. That her love discourse has had as yet no beginning is emphasised at the moment she speaks to Oenone in Act I, scene 3: 'Ciel! que lui vais-je dire? et par où commencer?' (l. 247)

With Phèdre, undifferentiated time is a refuge. Entering speech time is a disaster. In the case of Antiochus, it gives rise to anxiety because in this sort of time speech is absent. It is 'non-time' and therefore non-being. Silence has been imposed on him by Bérénice five years before the beginning of the action of the play. He enters speech time once he declares his love to Bérénice, thus punctuating this undifferentiated time. That love is only meaningful in speech emerges from his admission that, while he obeyed her injunction of silence: 'Mon cœur faisait serment de vous aimer sans cesse' (l. 208). His love was allowed no expression, an expression which was suppressed by the replacement of love discourse with another language, that of the friend and companion, thus a speech directed away from his love. The experience of this time was perceived as 'un éternel silence', thus representing un unpunctuated period of time, accompanied by existence in an 'unbroken' space: 'Dans l'Orient désert quel était mon ennui' (l. 234). Speech becomes necessary in order to punctuate this undifferentiated time even if it involves the suffering I have referred to earlier.

The theme of time without speech is one which occurs from almost the beginnings of Racinian tragedy. Ephestion reports to Cléofile what time has been like for Alexandre, for he has seen him: 'compter les tristes jours d'une longue absence' (l. 374). Such a time weighs heavily on the characters, but paradoxically, it is an abstract time, the time of day not the time of speech. But a form of undifferentiated time can occur within the action of a play, as *Bérénice* illustrates. Bérénice awaits the emergence of Titus from his period of mourning. Then he will return to the preoccupations of his love. But Bérénice waits in vain:

Ah! que cette longueur
D'un présage funeste épouvante mon cœur. (ll. 957–58)

Without the exchanges she is used to with Titus, time is unbroken. She is reduced to speaking to characters, such as Antiochus and her *confidente*, who are not central to her discourse of love.

Silence is by its very nature undifferentiated. As Xipharès explains: 'Cet amour s'est longtemps accru dans le silence' (l. 39). Moreover: 'Tout mon amour alors ne put pas éclater' (l. 197). 'Eclater' thus represents an end to undifferentiation, which, in this case, contains speech only in potential. It is only when Xipharès meets Monime after the reported death of his father that he enters speech time in the form of an exchange. This was not possible in her absence, a point reinforced by a spatial consideration:

[...] loin de vous, sans espoir de retour,
Je nourrissais encore un malheureux amour. (ll. 205–6)

Again, love is nothing without expression. It is through speech alone that characters fully achieve 'being' in love.

Often the end to undifferentiated time is explicitly mentioned by the characters and is once more related to silence. Acomat urges Roxane:

'Déclarons-nous, Madame, et rompons le silence' (l. 225) This can only happen once Roxane can see Bajazet in a real exchange, that is to say without the prior preparation of Atalide. Alexandre sees exchange, in terms of the direct expression of his love, as a contrast to the previous conditions of speech which had prevailed between himself and Cléofile:

> Combien de fois sensible à tes ardents désirs,
> M'est-il, en ta présence, echappé des soupirs!
> Mais je voulais encor douter de ma victoire:
> J'expliquais mes soupirs en faveur de la gloire. (ll. 979–82)

At this stage, then, he has had recourse to the discourse of reputation, another language of 'détournement'. Speaking of his love to her is referred to as 'rompre le silence' (l. 977). Ephestion explains what will now take place:

> Ce grand nom de vainqueur n'est plus ce qu'il souhaite;
> Il vient avec plaisir avouer sa défaite. (ll. 897–98)

He will then enter speech time, not the abstract and undifferentiated time of 'history'. As Titus, Bérénice and Antiochus will come to realise, history is non-being. It can only ever be 'reported' speech. Phèdre quite simply says, at the first stage of her confession: 'Je t'ai tout avoué' (l. 312) In her case the very act of speaking is sufficient to end a period of non-time. Oenone has heard 'ce que jamais on ne devait entendre' (l. 742). The 'on' is rather general here. The end to undifferentiated time will only be complete when she addresses Hippolyte as 'tu': 'De l'austère pudeur les bornes sont passées' (l. 766).

Undifferentiated time is very much a feature of the future for many characters. At the end of the plays characters pass from the being of speaking to the non-being of silence. This is the ultimate significance of the return to silence which I explored in Chapter 2. Antiochus emerges from undifferentiated time only to return to it (or so he thinks):

> Je me suis tu cinq ans,
> Madame, et vais encor me taire plus longtemps. (ll. 210–11)

For Monime, the return of Mithridate means that she must now 'jurer un silence éternel' (l. 698). Undifferentiated time will, as she thinks at that moment of the action, be reinstated. Love will have no future expression, as it has not had in the past. Her time with Mithridate would have been a sort of non-being since she would have had no meaningful speech with him. Indeed, interestingly, she accuses the king of having prevented her from taking refuge in this 'non-time':

Vous seul, Seigneur, vous seul, vous m'avez arrachée
A cette obéissance où j'étais attachée. (ll. 1339–40)

He alone has reactivated the discourse of love she had sworn to repress.

For Cléofile undifferentiated time as it stretches into the future is a time without exchange:

Songerez-vous, Seigneur, qu'une jeune princesse,
Au fond de ses Etats, vous regrette sans cesse? (ll. 921–22)

This reflects some aspects of undifferentiated time in the past in that the characters retreat into feelings which are not articulated in language. It is of course a time of silence, an end even to the sort of feelings Cléofile has just mentioned:

Hélas! s'il condamnait mes soupirs à se taire,
Que deviendrait alors ce cœur infortuné? (ll. 1310–11)

This question is most acutely addressed in *Bérénice*. Paulin attempts to persuade Titus to leave Bérénice on the grounds that a discourse other than that of love is possible:

Mais regardez plus loin: songez, en ce malheur,
Quelle gloire va suivre un moment de douleur. (ll. 1209–10)

But the idea of 'gloire' is fairly abstract compared with the history of speech which his love for Bérénice represents. Titus himself reflects upon his future in wondering how many days are left to him in order to fulfil himself as emperor: 'Sais-je combien le ciel m'a compté de journées?' (l. 1036) Again, however, this simple aggregate of days cannot compare with the individual days upon which each moment of speech with Bérénice was renewed. The most poignant expression of a future without speech is uttered by Bérénice herself:

Dans un mois, dans un an, comment souffrirons-nous,
Seigneur, que tant de mers me séparent de vous?
Que le jour recommence et que le jour finisse,
Sans que jamais Titus puisse voir Bérénice,
Sans que de tout le jour je puisse voir Titus? (ll. 1113–17)

Time like distance stretches endlessly into a future undifferentiated by speech, their past having been defined by that very speech. The experience of time as non-time will become for Titus 'un long bannissement' (l. 754) since he may be afflicted (which he was not) with 'une longue vie' (l. 756). Even in consolation the characters cannot escape the possibility of an absence of punctuation in time. Arsace, encouraging Antiochus not to give up hope in Act III, scene 4, cannot promise anything definite or defined:

> Laissez à ce torrent le temps de s'écouler
> Dans huit jours, dans un mois, n'importe, il faut qu'il passe.
> (ll. 942–43)

The future is a time without feelings articulated in language, of love without expression. Titus speaks of: 'Tout ce que j'aimerai jusqu'au dernier soupir' (l. 770). The most significant statement in this regard comes from Bérénice at the end of the play:

> J'ai cru que votre amour allait finir son cours,
> Je connais mon erreur, et vous m'aimez toujours. (ll. 1481–82)

This may very well be the case. Love may not be at an end, but the discourse of love will cease. The end of love discourse, moreover, is marked by the use of that crucial notation of finality: 'Pour la dernière fois, adieu, Seigneur' (l. 1506). The 'Hélas!' of Antiochus, so difficult to perform, represents the last, almost inarticulate gasp, before the three main characters recede into the non-existence of silence.

If, then, the characters' existence is defined by their place in a speech time, they have no raison d'être outside it. The transaction to be negotiated has to be spoken and the tragedy is constituted by a series of speech moments which may have emerged from the undifferentiated time I have just examined. However, I should like now to introduce a concept which, while not unrelated in some ways to undifferentiated time, is significantly distinct. I would like to argue that an essential aspect of the conditions of speech in Racinian tragedy is that characters can be 'out of time'.[4] The concept of being 'out of time' mostly arises rather once characters have entered speech time. Some characters may exclude others from speech time, in which case they are victims, or they may wish to avoid speech, to withdraw themselves from speech time. Being 'out of time' can therefore be an aspect of tragic status.

First, however, it is appropriate that the concept of being 'out of time' should be illustrated by scenes we do not see. In *Andromaque* it is intriguing that we do not witness the occasion on which Pyrrhus promises to save Astyanax and which takes place in the interval between the fourth and fifth acts. Why does Racine not consider this meeting appropriate to include in the speech time of Andromaque and Pyrrhus as presence in the stage space? Perhaps it is because it has no future or because there would be no real engagement on the part of Andromaque herself. It is out of time because she has already embarked on a course of action which is contrary to the expectation that Pyrrhus invests in the marriage. It would be a false conclusion. As it is, the pending marriage can be reported but overridden by Andromaque's intention to commit suicide.

Andromaque contains other meetings which are implied and not seen. Andromaque is, in Act I, scene 4, on her way to see Astyanax. But he does not exist as an individual, simply as an object of discussion and as a dramatic means to the end of the relationship between Pyrrhus and Andromaque herself. In any case he is perhaps less important even then, since, as many critics have pointed out, he is more symbolic of Andromaque's fidelity to Hector. Hence there is no need for him to figure in the speech time of the play. The lack of future in this axis of communication is further enhanced by Andromaque's desire to remove Astyanax to a deserted island, although this could also be a ploy to remove herself from speech time. Such isolation would obviate the need for exchange between the characters.

There are scenes we do not see in *Bajazet*. The most important one is the scene in which it seems that Bajazet has been reconciled with Roxane. One might imagine that Racine could have derived some dramatic value from such a meeting. But it turns out not to have been a real exchange, at least not one in which Bajazet has had to engage himself. Nothing has been said that has not already been said. It did not constitute the punctuation in time which Atalide was led to believe. Bajazet has not found a new voice: indeed his voice was not required.

One element in *Bajazet* which is worthy of comment is the use of the letter (I have already mentioned letters in my discussion of *Phèdre*). The letter is almost an equivalent of a scene we do not see because it is not stage speech. Bajazet sends a letter to Atalide informing her that he will never be able to pronounce words of love to Roxane (ll. 1142–44). The letter is later discovered by Roxane's *confidente* and presented to Roxane in Act IV, scene 5. It is out of time because the axis of communication has now shifted entirely to that between Bajazet and Roxane. There is no more future in exchanges between Bajazet and Atalide. Indeed these can be seen as a weakness in the play because they contribute little to the conclusion of the transaction. Atalide is redundant as a participant in speech time once Roxane has decided to speak to Bajazet alone. Atalide is a character virtually out of time, and reduced almost to non-being. Another letter is referred to in the play, and that is the letter from Amurat with which Roxane threatens Atalide and Bajazet in Act IV, scene 3. But

Amurat's letter in itself has little dramatic significance since the conclusion to the aspect of the transaction concerning Atalide and Bajazet is entirely dependent on the control Roxane has over dialogue in the play as a whole.

A 'non-stage' scene and a letter also form part of the action in *Iphigénie.* We are not witness to the occasion on which Eriphile reveals the attempted flight of Iphigénie and her mother (we learn about it in Act V, scene 1), which emphasises the non-time in which the character of Eriphile exists. Agamemnon also sends a letter to his wife and daughter in which he borrows Achille's voice in order to lure them to Aulis. The letter is out of time because it does not and could never form part of an exchange, and of course it is fraudulent. Agamemnon then writes a second letter telling them not to proceed to Aulis. This too is out of time because it constitutes in part an evasion; first, Agamemnon seeks to save his daughter from sacrifice, having already promised her life to the Greeks; secondly, he does not wish to reveal the real reason for his original letter. He desires above all to avoid a confrontation with his wife.

I have already referred to the characters' use of languages of 'détournement' in my discussion of undifferentiated time. Such languages perform a function once characters have punctuated undifferentiated time, since they have now entered speech time. Oenone urges Phèdre to adopt such a language once the death of Thésée has been 'confirmed', and to plead for her son in order to replace the discourse of love she has just enunciated (l. 340sq). This is an attempt to take Phèdre out of time, since, as we know, once the characters speak of love, they are unable to suppress similar utterances in the future. Indeed Phèdre tries hard in Act II, scene 5 to concentrate on the political succession to her husband but eventually breaks down. This is a belated attempt not to enter speech time with Hippolyte (l.586), the real object of her speech in the play. When Phèdre still harbours illusions of future discourse with Hippolyte, she looks for all sorts of reasons, in order to persuade him, which have no connection with love discourse itself. But this is a form of non-discourse, especially as it will be delivered not by Phèdre herself but by Oenone. It will not therefore form part of an exchange.

The plays contain other examples of attempts by characters, through the adoption of other languages, to take themselves out of the speech time which the characters have entered or must continue with. Hippolyte begins his meeting with Aricie entirely on a political note (l. 463sq) in order to avoid giving expression to his love. Later, once he has declared himself to Aricie and heard Phèdre's declaration of love, he attempts to take himself out of time by adopting an heroic language with his father. His revelation of the truth would in a way take him back into the speech time of Phèdre. Bajazet too seeks at all costs to extricate himself from the speech time he has been forced to enter with Roxane. He too attempts to adopt a political discourse, whereas Roxane desires quite another language (see l. 471sq).

The concept of alternative discourse affects Acomat, another Racinian character who finds himself outside the speech time of the other characters. Whereas the quality of being out of time is part of the tragic status of Antiochus, the position of Acomat reveals a singular weakness in the play. Certainly it is impossible to evacuate the political importance of the action in *Bajazet.* But there can be no question that the discourse of love is more central to the fate of the central characters. Acomat is only connected to the love intrigue tangentially. At the same time as offering her other forms of respect, he admits to Atalide:

> N'attendez point de moi ces doux emportements,
> Tels que j'en vois paraître au cœur de ces amants. (ll. 855–56)

At this point he is abruptly stopped in his tracks by Atalide: 'Vous m'en pourrez instruire avec le temps' (l. 861). Clearly, Atalide does not regard Acomat as participating in her own speech time. Nor can he be a part of the speech time of Roxane and Bajazet, although he has initiated it, and is directly affected by the future of that discourse. He is all the more unsatisfactory as a character for the fact that the two discourses of love and politics do not truly merge in the play. They are in different 'times'. Roxane may say to Acomat: 'Oui, vous serez content, je vais me déclarer' (l. 1341). But he recognises that she may not mean what he would wish her to mean. For him the love discourse has represented a means to an end in a time beyond it. For Roxane it has become the end itself.

Characters may also find themselves out of time by their exclusion from the discourse of others. Atalide cannot believe the change in Bajazet which has been suggested by his reconciliation with Roxane: 'Pourquoi de ce conseil moi seule suis-je excluse?' (l. 934) She fears that Bajazet has extracted himself from the speech time that they share. Agrippine has been taken out of time by Néron's constant evasions and by being reduced to speaking to relatively minor characters like Burrhus. This is non-discourse in the sense that Agrippine has to deal with intermediaries. It is not the sort of exchange that is required. One of the most remarkable speeches which finds itself out of time is that of

Agrippine in which she enumerates all her crimes. She has in fact just met with Néron so that in a sense the effect of this speech is already redundant. But at the same time the speech is not without effect because it marks the degree to which her power is now empty. The significance of the speech is that it has no significance.

Such is Antiochus's desire to remove himself from a speech time which is not his any more that he will not even hear the name of Bérénice mentioned (ll. 947–48). Indeed Antiochus is a classic case of exclusion, since his love discourse is not in the speech time of Bérénice and Titus:

> J'évite, mais trop tard,
> Ces cruels entretiens où je n'ai point de part. (ll. 272–23)

Another instance in *Bérénice* of being taken out of time is the silence in the love discourse of Titus after the end of his period of mourning. Bérénice is simply deprived of an interlocutor. This is especially insupportable given the previous regularity with which they have spoken. For Bérénice speech time would be restored even if she were only the subject of discourse. It is with a despairing voice that she asks Titus:

> Mais parliez-vous de moi quand je vous ai surpris?
> Dans vos secrets discours étais-je intéressée,
> Seigneur? Etais-je au moins présente à la pensée? (ll. 582–84)

Exclusion is also a feature of the speech conditions in a number of other Racinian tragedies. Néron recognises that he is unable to usurp the place of Britannicus in the speech time of Junie. The implication is that even if Néron were to succeed in keeping her with him, she would not participate in a real exchange. Junie would reduce him to non-being, his present state with Agrippine who has spoken for him, since Junie would have no meaningful speech to offer him. He has of course been 'present' during the meeting of Britannicus and Junie in which the latter was to break off all communication with the former. But he did not take the place of Britannicus:

> Eh bien! de leur amour tu vois la violence,
> Narcisse: elle a paru jusque dans son silence. (ll. 747–48)

Eventually, Junie destroys all possibility that Néron and she might share a speech time when she leaves his palace for the Vestal Virgins.

It is the fate of Mithridate to be excluded from the speech time of Monime. He returns from defeat with the intention of taking up with Monime as he had left off, although precisely what that situation was is not made entirely clear in the play. He finally discovers that Monime is in love with Xipharès and that his place in her speech time has been usurped. But is it really a case of usurpation? In the first place the anteriority of the love of Xipharès and Monime suggests otherwise. Their speech time is a belated one, but it could have taken place in any case, but it so happened that Mithridate thwarted its beginning. In the second place, it is constantly emphasised in the play that Xipharès is the worthy successor to Mithridate to the point of being 'un autre moi-même'. Thus it is entirely appropriate that Mithridate should make a gift of Monime to his faithful son at the end of the play. In so doing he legitimises a speech time in which he had no part.

In *Andromaque* exclusion is a recurrent aspect of the speech conditions of the play, since each of the women is excluded in their turn. The effect is not the same in each case. Andromaque does all she can to exclude herself from the speech time of Pyrrhus. Their common subject of discourse is however Astyanax. Eventually Andromaque is drawn into a real exchange with Pyrrhus because it is only in such an exchange that the promise to save her son can be made. As I have observed earlier, we are not witness to this scene, and in this way Racine preserves Andromaque's desire to be 'out of time'. Her real speech time is with the dead Hector whom she consults at his tomb. In this sense she and Pyrrhus can never share the same time.

The situation with Hermione is clear enough. Her natural speech time is with Pyrrhus who resists being drawn into it, just as Andromaque resists being drawn into the speech time of Pyrrhus. It is significant again that we do not see the one reconciliation of Hermione and Pyrrhus in the play. Indeed Pyrrhus charges Oreste to inform her that he will honour his promise to marry her, although by the time Oreste sees her in Act III, scene 2, she already knows (l. 807). Moreover, Pyrrhus intends to meet Hermione in Act III, scene 6 but fatally meets Andromaque instead. The reconciliation with Hermione never reaches the stage of being an exchange. Their only meeting in the last scene of Act IV is the last word in exclusion since Pyrrhus utters the cruelly dismissive: 'Rien ne vous engageait à m'aimer en effet' (l. 1355). He effectively implies that for him, she has no 'being' in the sense that love could never have provided a shared discourse between them. A speech time has simply never existed for them. Significantly, therefore, he remains silent when Hermione pleads that he delay the wedding by a day. She accuses him of thinking of someone else, that is to say of being in another time, a time which actually does not exist. On the other hand, Hermione shows herself not to be above excluding Oreste from her speech time, a speech time she claims to desire:

> Mais qui sait si depuis
> Je n'ai point en secret partagé vos ennuis? (ll. 523–24)

Or again:

> Enfin, qui vous a dit que malgré mon devoir
> Je n'ai pas quelquefois souhaité de vous voir? (ll. 527–28)

Oreste is not fooled and realises that he is not participating in a real exchange: 'Le cœur est pour Pyrrhus, et les vœux pour Oreste' (l. 538). He discovers in Act V how he has never had a place in her speech time. She has promised herself as the reward for killing Pyrrhus, but even at the last moment she wishes to communicate with him through Oreste. He in turn takes her speech out of time by not delivering it, and Pyrrhus thinks he is being killed for political reasons. In any case, Oreste should never have believed that she intended to kill him, which suggests that, in giving the order, she was never really addressing Oreste. Oreste is a character whose speech is destined to be entirely out of time.

Phèdre seems to move in and out of speech time. As in the case of Antiochus, Oenone's position of messenger gives rise to a certain number of problems. In order for the strategy of concealment to succeed, Phèdre must take herself out of speech time altogether: 'Mon zèle n'a besoin que de votre silence' (l. 894). But Phèdre decides to take herself back into speech time by going to intercede with Thésée on Hippolyte's behalf. Oenone's plan was in part to suppress the discourse of love by isolating Phèdre from the occasions on which it might resurface. Her meeting with Thésée reactivates that discourse because she discovers that Hippolyte is in love with Aricie and that she is for ever excluded from the speech time of Hippolyte which she has hoped to enter. Phèdre then finds herself on her own, since her reproachful attitude towards Oenone leads the latter to commit suicide. Phèdre only finds her voice once she is prepared to speak (rather than write) the truth. It is ironic that her last speech moment should be with Thésée whose speech time she naturally shares. It is their sole moment of exchange in the play, for their first ends in the hurried exit of Phèdre and their second never achieves the purpose she intends.

I have now analysed speech in relation to time in the past and as a present. In addition speech at any given moment in the action implies the possibility of a future, especially since every character looks forward to the transaction coming to a conclusion of some sort. It is perhaps in this investment of the characters in the future of their speech, and the way speech in the present undermines that future, that the tragic quality of acts of speech truly resides.

One element which ensures speech in the future is the prospect of revelation. The solitary expression of love is never sufficient for it must be conveyed to the object of that love. Xipharès, in respect of Monime, talks of 'l'aveu que je prétends lui faire' (l. 104). The process of revelation is given new impetus when Pharnace hints to Mithridate that 'Xipharès, Seigneur, ne vous a pas tout dit' (l. 994). Although Roxane controls the beginning and end of dialogue, she too needs to maintain the conditions of speech if she is to have a hope of hearing what she wants to hear. This is constantly projected into the future. On Acomat's insistence that she declare her hand, she replies that she will not do so until she has seen Bajazet personally (ll. 254–55). At each stage and after each negative response, interspersed with one false reconciliation, she needs to reassure herself that there is no further prospect of love from him. The discovery of the letter prompts her to attempt one last effort but Bajazet himself confirms that the process is at an end.

Speech concerning Eriphile is entirely in the future in the sense that the revelation of her identity, which she is anxious to know herself, provides a solution to the problem of Agamemnon. But Eriphile herself has no real interlocutors since she refuses to reveal her love to Achille. While the mystery of her identity projects the play into the future, her dialogue in itself has no future. The forward process of *Athalie* is entirely dependent on the moment at which Joad decides to reveal the identity of Eliacin. It is the mystery surrounding his identity which prompts the intervention of the queen and which provides the conditions of speech of all the characters.

Thus expectation, so much a part of the structure of Racinian drama, prolongs the conditions in which speech is possible. Hermione, we are informed by Pylade:

> [...] croit que trop heureux de fléchir sa rigueur
> Il (= Pyrrhus) la viendra presser de reprendre son cœur.
> (ll. 127–28)

Phèdre entertains hopes that she will be able to resume communication with Hippolyte: 'Cherchons pour l'attaquer quelque endroit plus sensible' (ll. 794). Oreste is led to hope that Hermione will resume dialogue with him: 'Quelquefois elle appelle Oreste à son secours' (l. 132). What is at stake here is continuity. Nowhere is this more true than of *Bérénice.* Bérénice will seek out Titus:

> [...] et dans cette entrevue
> Dire tout ce qu'aux cœurs l'un de l'autre contents
> Inspirent des transports retenus si longtemps. (ll. 324–26)

From the breakdown of this continuity Antiochus sees the chance of future dialogue with Bérénice: 'Je jouirai longtemps de ses chers entretiens' (l. 789). But as Antiochus quickly realises, expectation may be a feeling without a future. Equally, at the very moment that Agamemnon can no longer speak to Iphigénie as his daughter, she expects the natural discourse between father and daughter to resume without difficulty and is surprised when it does not (l. 558sq).

In general terms the future of dialogue or speech is always vulnerable since, as we have observed, there are characters who have the power to bring it to an end. While Andromaque may not wish to be drawn into speech with Pyrrhus, she needs it to continue if she is to stand any chance of saving her son. That is her paradox. The future of dialogue for Hermione is constantly threatened by the presence of Andromaque. In her case (and for other reasons in the case of Oreste) it turns out to be an illusion. Néron wishes desperately to secure a basis for the future of his own speech which has been so much associated with the past and with Agrippine. He ends up without a discourse at all, because he has alienated his mother and lost Junie. In *Bérénice* we witness the growing awareness on the part of the characters that dialogue between them has absolutely no future, something made clear from the very beginning with the example of Antiochus. At all stages of the tragedies, there are characters who attempt to lay the foundations for future dialogue and those who resist that process.

The possibility of dialogue in the future is thrown into doubt if one of the parties to the exchange wishes to avoid the conclusion that is necessary to the transaction which is being negotiated. Andromaque will not interrupt her 'silence' in the sense that she will not tell Pyrrhus what he requires to hear. He reminds her:

> Sa grâce à vos désirs pouvait être accordée;
> Mais vous ne l'avez pas seulement demandée. (ll. 909–10)

In the same way Hermione avoids the conclusion that Oreste wants to reach, namely her departure from Epire.

The problem of securing dialogue for the future may be exacerbated by a disjunction in the 'time' of the speech of the respective characters. Atalide has clearly deluded herself into thinking that speech with Bajazet has a future. She has believed that the present could be endlessly renewed, whereas the real future lay anyway in the dialogue of Roxane and Bajazet. Exchanges between Néron and his mother have no future because she retains him in the past of which their exchanges would simply be a replication. In order to discover a new voice to rid himself of that past, he needs a new interlocutor and finds her in Junie. She in her turn refers to that past which Néron instantly resents (l. 563sq, ll. 603–18 and ll. 627–32), since Junie is intended to be the means of establishing his future voice.

The characters themselves are sometimes aware that their speech has no future. Axiane complains: 'Mais que sert de pousser des soupirs superflus?' (l. 991) Antiochus is aware of the inopportune timing of his first declaration for five years:

> Dois-je croire qu'au rang où Titus la destine
> Elle m'écoute mieux que dans la Palestine? (ll. 27–28)

He is allowed later to dream of a future but it is an illusion that does not last long. Even if there is a future in speech, there is no future in being ignored.

Occasions arise when no grounds at all exist for future dialogue. Such is the case with the curious meeting between Hermione and Andromaque in Act III, scene 4. Its sole object is Andromaque's plea for Hermione to intercede with Pyrrhus. Indeed there are no grounds in the past for this dialogue, although Andromaque attempts to evoke the historical precedent of Hector, on the insistence of his wife, acting to protect Helen. The two speeches have no status in time beyond the present. Mithridate's plan to march on Rome almost falls into the same category since it will have no consequences in action, although it leads to the arrest of Pharnace, and is a monologue within dialogue. Essentially, the plan exists only in speech and has only a present.

Future speech or dialogue may in addition be imperilled by the elimination of the conditions which would allow it. Agrippine and Britannicus gradually find themselves without interlocutors. Pallas is banished (l. 361sq) and Octavie is repudiated (l. 467sq). Clearly for effective exchange to take place, access must not be denied to the characters. Agrippine, in her momentous interview with Néron in Act IV, scene 3 demands: 'Que vous me permettiez de vous voir à toute heure'

(l. 1282). Of course, as we know, Néron's new voice depends on the elimination of other voices. Speaking of his plan to murder Britannicus, Néron exclaims:

C'en est trop: il faut que sa ruine
Me délivre à jamais des fureurs d'Agrippine. (ll. 1305–6)

If discontinuity constitutes a major feature of Racinian discourse, this discontinuity is further enhanced by the interruptive function that some of the characters or events perform in the plays. Mithridate's return, and his expected resumption of dialogue with Monime, momentarily at least, remove any possibility of future dialogue between Xipharès and Monime. The latter indeed sends Xipharès away to avoid any prospect that she will reiterate her love for him. Eriphile's function is entirely interruptive, even in the way she provides the solution to the problem of the oracle. She dreams of setting Agamemnon against Achille and of destroying Iphigénie (ll. 1130–36 and l. 1488). She herself grabs the knife and slits her own throat (ll. 1771–72). Thésée's arrival in Trézène can only be interruptive to the love discourse of Phèdre with Hippolyte (this is entirely illusory of course) and that of Hippolyte and Aricie. He also brings down the curse on Hippolyte which ensures that he and Aricie do not reach the temple to swear their union to the gods. Oenone too performs a sort of interruptive function in that she prevents the emergence of the truth until it is too late.

But it is sometimes implied that dialogue can be projected beyond the end of the action of the play. In the first place characters speak of the way in which others will talk about them once they are gone. Monime projects discourse into the future on an historical level in the expectation that she will die. What is said about her will be all that remains:

Retourne maintenant chez ces peuples heureux,
Et, si mon nom encor s'est conservé chez eux,
Dis-leur ce que tu vois, et de toute ma gloire,
Phoedime, conte-leur la malheureuse histoire. (ll. 1529–32)

The characters themselves will no longer be the producers of speech in the future but the subjects of it.

Similarly the situation that Iphigénie finds herself in, namely that her death will be the source of Achille's future reputation, will be the beginning of 'le récit d'une si belle histoire' (ll. 1555–58). Indeed the thought of a place in history is used as a means of persuasion in the case of Agamemnon. Ulysse tempts the king with a graphic description of their future victory, which will be 'l'éternel entretien des siècles à venir' (l. 388). In a sense this is 'out of time' for Agamemnon since he knows that such a picture cannot be part of the speech time that he has to enter with his wife and daughter. Ulysse's attempt is thus rendered futile.

The persuasion of a future time when the characters will be the favourable subject of the discourse of others features too in *Britannicus.* Burrhus exhorts Néron to think of what people say of him now and how rewarding it will be if this can be projected into the future (l. 1349sq). Indeed Néron himself is concerned about how people will speak of him. If I embark on the road to tyranny: 'de tout l'univers quel sera le langage?' (l. 1417) Titus hopes to reduce himself to a subject of discourse in view of the fact that Bérénice must leave: 'Que mon nom soit toujours dans tous vos entretiens' (l. 762). He says this to a character who is leaving Rome because he can stand no longer the repetition of Titus's name. But all these examples have a tragic quality in that they deny the presence of the characters necessary for the performance of the speech they might wish to share with others they love.

Being the subject of discourse is something that exercises the mind of the characters in *Phèdre.* Phèdre is anxious about what her children will hear about her:

> Je tremble qu'un discours, hélas! trop véritable,
> Un jour ne leur reproche une mère coupable. (ll. 865–66)

In addition she fears meeting her father in the underworld when she will be:

> Contrainte d'avouer tant de forfaits divers,
> Et des crimes peut-être inconnus aux enfers. (ll. 1283–84)

The pain of this particular discourse in the future is that she will have to reiterate a confession which has already caused her so much suffering. Her crimes may be unheard of, so that the horror of saying such things to an unsuspecting audience will replicate her experience as it is represented in the play. Finally, Hippolyte is afraid that no conditions of speech will be available to him after his banishment. He will have no interlocutors in the future:

> Chargé du crime affreux dont vous me soupçonnez,
> Quels amis me plaindront, quand vous m'abandonnez?
> (ll. 1144–45)

But what speech conditions can really be envisaged beyond the action of the play? What are the conditions of speech for the characters who remain? In one or two plays, of course no character of note remains alive so that dialogue is at an end in an absolute sense. The most important example of this is *Bajazet*, where Roxane has Bajazet killed, upon which Atalide commits suicide, and Roxane is killed herself. Acomat remains, but is not of sufficient tragic status for this to matter. *Bajazet* also illustrates another important aspect of language beyond the play in that Roxane, in killing Bajazet, removes any prospect whatsoever of speech in the future. The same problem can be identified with Hermione who kills, with Pyrrhus, any possibility that he will return to a discourse of love. But in *Andromaque*, as we shall see, there are characters left to tell the tale. Not in *La Thébaïde*, since all the main characters die. The situation is not quite the same as that of *Bajazet* in that, from the beginning of the play, no common ground, except that of family ties, exists between the characters. This is the essence of its weakness as a play.

In *Andromaque* the widow of Hector does not commit suicide and her son is saved. That axis of communication, such as it is, continues. In any case Andromaque had laid plans as if she were going to die. She charges Céphise not to follow her in death, for she will be Pyrrhus's interlocutor in her stead (ll. 1107–12). Interestingly, this coninues the non-discourse that has prevailed in the course of the play since how can a mere *confidente* replace a character of more exalted rank? Indeed it is of further note that the non-discourse between Pyrrhus and Andromaque continues at the wedding ceremony: 'Sans joie et sans murmure elle semble obéir' (l. 1440). Moreover Astyanax is at that moment isolated, 'Dans un fort éloigné du temple et du palais' (l. 1456). Communication simply falls apart at the end of the play. Even Andromaque's survival does not necessarily constitute a future. She may command, but the reason for her previous communication has now been removed. She is free but has no dialogue except with her son. Oreste of course too lives on. But there are no grounds for dialogue between him and Andromaque, as is evidenced by the fact that they never meet in the play. The two separate worlds of the tragedy continue in isolation one from the other. It is debatable whether this is a strength or a weakness of *Andromaque* as a tragedy.

In *Bérénice* the absence of communication in the future constitutes the whole of the characters' tragedy. Whereas in the case of Titus and Bérénice speech had filled their time, now it will be silence. Titus may reign but it will be in an undifferentiated world, that of Rome. Titus almost never talks of reigning as emperor in terms of a personally lived experience. He views it in terms of history and duty, what Rome expects. It is external to himself. Rome will be the equivalent of the desert to which Bérénice will return, an empty space without interlocutors. For Antiochus Rome has always been an empty space, in a sense extending the desert from which he has emerged. He has spoken to Bérénice and Titus but not using his own voice. His tragedy is that, even in speech, he has been without real interlocutors. At the end of *Bérénice* the two men no longer have grounds for dialogue with the queen or with each other.

Andromaque and *Bérénice* provide a category of play which sees an end to repetition and therefore to speech itself. Finality is not altered in any way by Andromaque's survival for the reasons I have mentioned. On the other hand there is a group of plays where, despite appearances, no such finality marks the end of the tragic action. Nowhere is this more so than in *Mithridate* where Xipharès and Monime are permitted to envisage a future of shared discourse. The situation could even be considered one of continuity where Xipharès takes the place of Mithridate. But this would be misleading. It is obvious that Xipharès is morally superior to his father. He has always acted honourably with Monime, which is not the case with his father who desired a sexual union with Monime without offering marriage (ll. 49–52). He was also in love with Monime before his father had even heard of her. It is therefore a new and qualitatively distinct discourse of love that he enters into with Monime. *Mithridate* represents a break with the discourse of the past.[5]

In *Iphigénie* too Racine allows two characters who love each other to envisage a future of shared discourse. Iphigénie herself is spared from the sacrifice and returned to Achille, who is also reconciled with Agamemnon:

> Des mains d'Agamemnon venez la recevoir.
> Venez: Achille et lui, brûlant de vous revoir,
> Madame, et désormais tous deux d'intelligence,
> Sont prêts à confirmer leur auguste alliance. (ll. 1787–90)

Racine obviously inserts a 'cultural' irony into the play in that, while in the play the grounds for future discourse are laid between the characters, his audience knows that another perspective on the behaviour of Achilles is available to them. But irrespective of that, the words I have just quoted are addressed to Clytemnestre whose last speech in the play expresses gratitude for the actions of Achille. She is conspicuously silent about any possibility that relations between her and her husband will be restored. Again this looks forward to other episodes in the life of this couple which Racine's audience would have been aware of.

The full tragedy of the speech situation beyond the action of the play, perhaps the crowning quality of *Bérénice*, is also to be found in *Phèdre* but in a different way. Hippolyte and Aricie are not permitted to envisage a future of dialogue together. For Phèdre no dialogue is possible beyond the revelation of the truth, which she has allowed to be concealed, a revelation which is therefore a fitting end to her own discourse. She has no way out but suicide. Thésée too has been deprived of the possibility of dialogue both with his wife and with his son. But it is suggested in the play that that is not the end of all speech. For, as I have explained in the context of voice and substitution, Aricie becomes a replacement for his son, or a form of expiation for Hippolyte's death:

> Que malgré les complots d'une injuste famille
> Son amante aujourd'hui me tienne lieu de fille. (ll. 1653–54)

The tragedy is that the restoration of some form of communication is only possible after suffering, and tragedy is nothing if not knowledge through suffering. Indeed, what is required at the end of *Phèdre* is a new language, a new language that begins with the end of the play. Racine envisages a new future for speech, radically different from the old, where Thésée and Aricie have been isolated one from the other. The situations in *Andromaque* and *Phèdre* are thus totally reversed.

What of the plays I have not mentioned so far? Alexandre finds himself in the ironical position of envisaging a future without Cléofile who herself must live without Alexandre and her brother: 'Je ne puis que me taire et pleurer mes ennuis' (l. 1544). Equally ironically, it is Porus and Axiane, previously the enemies of Alexandre, who can look forward to a life together. But the focus of their dialogue is less clear, since throughout the play the issues of politics and love have never merged with any real success. *Esther* and *Athalie* (a new language for Racine after *Phèdre*) represent the reestablishment of a certain discourse. In the case of the latter David's line is reestablished and the interruptive discourse of Athalie (a new religion) is eliminated. Joad's prophecy certainly suggests that problems on the human level remain but there is no doubt that God's word, for doubters like Abner, is never silent. Esther's action ensures that the voice of the Jews as a people is also never silenced.

Britannicus appears to be more pessimistic as regards the future of speech. Clearly the rift between Néron and his mother is unbridgeable. Nor has Néron succeeded in establishing his new voice becuse he has now been deprived of the interlocutor who would have been the addressee of that voice. Is speech however at an end? One speech is reported at the end of the tragedy which may be intended to point to a possible future. Junie addresses the statue of Augustus, thus suggesting that one form of discourse can survive beyond the period of Néron. It is however a general discourse which does not form part of interpersonal discourse. Is there not a further irony in that it is precisely the adoption of this discourse which will constitute Titus's personal tragedy, especially since Bérénice has cured him of the decadence contracted by being brought up in Nero's court?

Time in Racinian tragedy is built into speech and is a constituent element of the tension of utterance. Characters are aware of the pressures and commitments of speech in the past. But speech in the present is fragile. Characters do not know whether this or the next speech will be their last. Hence their anxiety, all too often founded, for the possibility of speech in the future. So time is not an abstract in the plays. It is not even a 'unity'. Speech is time, and time is speech. Its discontinuity is often disunity.

Conclusion

In this study I have attempted to indicate where, in the context of tragedy, focusing attention on acts of speech might lead us in our interpretation of Racine's plays, and in particular my aim has been to demonstrate the extent to which the plays can be regarded as plays about language. In this perspective the choice that is imposed on the characters is linguistic in nature. A 'yes' or a 'no' must be pronounced, something the characters find singularly difficult. It must also be heard. Failure to pronounce leads to dire consequences. Characters can moreover choose wrongly. Again that choice is consequential, as Hermione and Phèdre in particular discover. But wrong choices are made because of the pressures of a *situation* where characters must face others who demand speech of them. The act of speech is thus paramount. It is in this sense therefore that, in the words of Yves Pihan: 'Racine semble avoir révélé que le problème de l'expression dépasse de beaucoup celui du langage et cela donne à son oeuvre une dimension nouvelle, une résonance très moderne' (p. 55).

It is for this reason that I have concentrated particularly on the notion of voice. The characters' knowledge of what they must say, their awareness of the consequences that will ensue from such pronouncements, makes speech a singularly difficult act, and contributes in a direct way to the tragic effect. It is often the movement from speech to silence, the crossing of a frontier which can be defined in terms of 'voicing', of articulating that which was concealed in the obscurity of silence, that the initiative for tragedy is born. It is appropriate therefore that Barthes describes speech in *Phèdre* as 'accouchement'. It is a metaphor appropriate for the whole of Racinian drama.

This view of Racinian tragedy would tend to lead us away from an interpretation that rests primarily on notions of psychology in that it addresses what happens to characters in a *situation*. Speech as communication between individuals, as Michael Hawcroft has convincingly demonstrated in terms of acts of persuasion,[1] is what the characters have to attend to, not an 'inner space' of which that speech is a representation. Although it may be felt that discussions of psychology are old hat, the description of Racinian tragedy as psychological is a tenacious tradition, not least because it survives through a pedagogy which is reluctant to abandon the concept and in texts of criticism which have otherwise great value in their insights.[2] It would be tedious to re-rehearse all the arguments against it. It could be held however that in drama, and in Racinian tragedy even above all, characters are not paraded for our inspection. In terms of the drama there is no inner life. There is on the other hand speech. Characters exist to do things and they do them in Racine by speaking. Speaking is a form of protection and a form of violence, to oneself and to others.

According to this interpretation, the interface of the characters with the world is through language, and it is through dialogue, in other words with others, that we engage in the world. It is *telling* others about ourselves and our feelings for them. It is the ultimate and inescapable requirement to explicate that can lead to consequences of the greatest importance. Equally the refusal to explicate places characters in a situation of great peril. Subjectivity within the context of character can no longer be isolated because it is always related to a response.

My account of the experience of Racinian tragedy therefore might suggest that that experience does not need to be located in transcendance of any sort, be it psychological or religious. We do not have to posit invisible worlds or orders, like the space of the 'mind' of which we see only a part or any determinisms beyond the characters such as fate, in order to construct the full impact of humanity in the midst of awesome difficulty. The principal quality of the Racinian tragic experience would rather lie therefore in the here and now, in the immanence of linguistic choices, in the realisation that those choices have consequences for one's own life or the lives of others, that existence or death can depend on a word. In my introduction I described that as a simple but powerful concept. In this context the problem of whether the gods really exist for Phèdre or whether they are a metaphor for her guilt is a problem of a second order. It is not a problem of speech itself.

All this helps us perhaps to resolve that perennial dichotomy between drama as literature and as theatre, so much a problem in Racinian tragedy where action in the conventional sense of the term seems to be lacking. What then is *theatrical* about Racinian tragedy? David Maskell has attempted to respond to traditional notions of action in Racine's plays by drawing up an impressive list of all types of physical movement both implicit and explicit in the texts. On this level his discussion of theatricality is highly successful. Problems arise when Maskell deals with the relation between the verbal and the visual, at which point he seems to hesitate between different ideas. At times the visual is an adjunct to the verbal. At others some claim appears to be made for the independence of physical movement where the word is to some degree effaced: 'the words play a subordinate role' (p. 162). He argues further that: 'Speech and action usually perform jointly in Racinian drama, but sometimes one will step back and the other take the limelight' (p. 246).

Maskell complains that those aspects of Racinian theatricality which have been explored in the past 'have been treated in isolation, rather than as part of a coherent theatrical system' (p. 131). This is certainly true, but I question whether, in terms of speech in Racine, Maskell has provided us with an adequate answer. His most problematic statement is that: 'Racine's characters seldom merely talk about their emotions and feelings: they embody them in action, often in physical action. Racine crossed the frontier into true theatrical territory' (p. 185). My principal objection to this position is the implication that language is not enough to sustain theatricality, that a physical dimension beyond language acts as an essential support in order to enter this 'true theatrical territory'.

Racine locates theatre precisely in matters of language. They do not obviously eliminate a physical dimension, but the physical dimension in Racine is primarily the voice. Characters must choose to voice their thoughts and feelings, hence my preference of 'vocal' over Maskell's 'verbal'. They may move at the same time, but that is a secondary feature of Racine's theatricality. The text, in its emphasis on the problematics of speaking and listening, carries within it the demand to be *spoken* for it makes no sense otherwise. Voice is presence. The text contains in other words the principles of its own articulation, and it is in this sense that Racine's tragedies offer a *systematic* exploitation of the word. That is the coherence of Racinian theatricality. The text is performance, all of which takes us beyond Racine as 'literary' theatre.

Is it then possible to look at the theatricality of Racinian tragedy in a wider perspective and to identify within Racine's tragic order a reflexion on the activity of theatre itself? Several elements of the plays suggest that this might be the case. In the first place, the importance ascribed to expectation in speech coincides with the idea of the stage as above all a place of presence, but more than that, a place where presence is marked by speech. On the whole, an audience expects a stage to be filled and to be filled with people talking (in this sense mime in itself is spectacle not theatre). An unpopulated space eventually becomes the arena where the frontier between speech and silence is crossed. Actors break a silence in precisely the way Racinian characters do. Racine foregrounds, in the problematics of listening and speaking as I have described it, the situation of theatre itself. And he achieves this further through the demand of presence which is built into the relationships of the characters. They demand to be satisfied through speech. For one character that speech must come from another with whom he or she is most closely engaged in the transaction at the centre of the drama. No intermediary will do. Anything else is simply the equivalent of the empty space with which the performance begins. The spectators' and the characters' demands combine in this way to form the dynamics of the action.

A concomitant of presence is the notion of absence as denial. The failure of the performance to begin is a deprivation, because no response is possible. The transaction between the characters, and that which is at the centre of the relationship of the spectator to the theatre, is at an end. There is no Racinian tragedy, as there is no theatre, without voice. In positing the possibility of the absence of voice, the stage and the characters become void of being. In a sense deprivation of voice is built into the dialogue of the characters through the denial of expectation. Even while the characters are present in that they appear on the stage together, the failure of one to respond in the desired way to the other is a denial, in effect an absence. But this concept of absence is only possible if Racine projects at the same time a strong view of theatre and of speech as presence as a basic principle of the drama.

The place of the audience in relation to the stage is further projected into the tragedies through the concept of performance which is certainly the central focus of Racine's reflection on the experience of theatre. Simply, the characters' problems are actors' problems. That is to say that both characters and actors have to make choices regarding the performance of the words they must speak: they have to convince an audience. This is all the more crucial since actors and characters face their critics, and a critique of performance is being enacted on both sides of the curtain. All are concerned with their reception by others.

Another aspect of performance which the actor and the character share is that they are brought from obscurity into light. The space of the stage and what it represents are made real through exposure. Marc Fumaroli makes this point in relation to *Phèdre*:

> Autant d'images classiques, renvoyant au théâtre comme dévoilement dans la lumière, et l'identifiant au passage solennel du personnage, de la nuit et de l'absence à son éclatante apparition sur la scène illuminée. Avec Phèdre qui s'avance sur la scène, c'est le théâtre même qui dans ce mouvement se résume et se réfléchit. Une seconde série de métaphores, celle de l'aveu sur fond de rétraction et de silence, complète la définition métaphorique du théâtre: il est genèse non seulement du visible mais du verbe.[3]

Junie, Roxane, Bajazet and others are part of the same phenomenon. It is, of course, the same for the actor. Once on stage, a commitment to the performance is made. It cannot be interrupted, in the same way that characters are ineluctably trapped in the momentum of speech which they often in any case fail to control once the barrier between silence and speech has been crossed. The actor is propelled into a space where he must keep going, while paradoxically portraying the choice between speech or non-speech. Equally, the vehicle of voice on the stage must at times act out the deprivation of voice.

But Racine's theatre is also a challenge to the actor. As we have observed, the characters' performance often breaks down. Hermione cannot act the woman in love with Oreste. Bajazet is unable to speak as the convincing lover of Roxane. Phèdre finds it impossible to sustain the role of the pleading mother in front of Hippolyte. The theme of substitution both within and between characters points up the discontinuity of language which seems to characterise Racinian tragedy. But this breakdown or discontinuity is denied the actor from whom a unity of performance is required. The actor (ruling out any sort of Brechtian performance) cannot betray himself as an actor, although paradoxically he must play the character as actor, as performer.

Most of all, however, Racine's tragedies represent 'being' through language in a particular space. The characters themselves are not disembodied minds moving about in each other's inner space. Most significant, however, is Racine's reflexion on the actor. The actor's being is invested in his presence on the stage. His function in society is performance, and moreover performance as a form of sacrifice, because that being is an ephemeral being. It is discontinuous. It is a permanent form of substitution. The being of the actor is thus encapsulated in a form of theatre which itself foregrounds above all discontinuity. The lot of the actor is to help us comprehend a certain experience of language, a tragic experience of language. In this sense Racine is certainly a playwright for modern times.

Notes

Notes to Introduction.

1 All the titles related to the authors mentioned here and to the names of authors that follow are to be found in the Selective Bibliography. The absence of reference to Richard Parish's monograph is due to the fact that his work appeared after the text of my book had largely been produced. It is especially gratifying to note that he frequently arrives at conclusions very similar to my own but from a different perspective.

2 All references are to the Garnier edition of Racine's plays, edited by Jacques Morel and Alain Viala (Paris, 1980).

Notes to Chapter 1

1 Jacques Scherer notes that: 'La parole n'est pas que la parole. Elle peut avoir pour conséquence des faits redoutables', *Racine et / ou la cérémonie* (Paris, 1982), p.67.

2 The notion of desire is an important component of drama for Ubersfeld: 'La détermination du sujet ne peut se faire que par rapport à l'action, et dans une corrélation avec un objet. A proprement parler, il n'y a pas de sujet autonome dans un texte, mais *un axe sujet-objet.* Nous dirions alors qu'est sujet dans un texte littéraire, ce ou celui autour du *désir* de qui l'action, c'est-à-dire le modèle actantiel s'organise, celui que l'on peut prendre pour sujet de la phrase actantielle, celui dont la positivité du désir avec les obstacles qu'elle rencontre entraîne le mouvement de tout le texte' (*Lire le théâtre* (Paris, 1982), p.72). For the development of this idea, see pp.71–97.

3 A view of Racinian discourse which sees conflict at the centre of the tragedies is provided by Ingrid Heyndels for whom characters in the tragedies do not argue at all, since they never achieve 'le contact des esprits' necessary for minimal interpersonal comprehension. This contact depends on a 'domaine de l'argumentation' where the essential criteria are '(le) vraisemblable, (le) plausible, (le) probable' (*Le Conflit racinien: Esquisse d'un système tragique* (Brussels, 1985), pp.242–44). These criteria, she suggests, are never met by the characters.

4 It might be useful to mention here H. P. Grice's 'cooperative principle' quoted by Andrew Kennedy: 'Our talk exchanges do not normally consist of disconnected remarks, and would not be rational if they did. They are characteristically, to some degree at least, cooperative efforts; and each participant recognises in them, to some extent, a common purpose or set of purposes, or at least a mutually acceptable direction'

(*Dramatic Dialogue* (Cambridge, 1983), p.9). Kennedy argues that for the purposes of studying dramatic dialogue, such a principle provides us with 'a judgement of "an angle of deviation"' (p.10).

5 Catherine Spencer argues that the basis of Mithridate's desire for shared discourse with Monime is recognition: 'un accord, un consentement sans lequel l'hymen qui s'apprête est nul et sans valeur' (*La Tragédie du Prince: Etude du personnage médiateur dans le théâtre tragique de Racine* (Paris — Seattle — Tübingen, 1987), p.438).

6 For Ubersfeld: 'tout énoncé ne fonctionne dans un échange que si les deux interlocuteurs se sont mis d'accord, implicitement, sur un certain nombre de *présupposés*' (*Lire*, p.279). The tragedies of Racine are often based on the illusory nature of such 'présupposés'.

7 Spencer has the following to say on the possibility of shared discourse between Pyrrhus and Andromaque: 'La nouveauté de Pyrrhus, ce qui donne à la requête de la reconnaissance une intensité jusque-là inconnue, c'est qu'il figure un héros déchiré, qui se renie lui-même et implore de l'élue, non seulement un nouveau règne, mais surtout une nouvelle identité, un présent neuf, un avenir vierge' (p.498).

Notes to Chapter 2

1 Maskell comments on the irony created by the entwined initials of Titus and Bérénice and the nature of what is said during the course of the action (p.26).

2 Spencer realises the significance of the complementary nature of 'parler et se montrer' (p.56). Judd D. Hubert's comment on *Phèdre* is appropriate also to *Britannicus*: 'C'est qu'un rôle ne peut vraiment se manifester publiquement et sortir pour ainsi dire de la coulisse, qu'en se verbalisant, tout au moins en ce qui concerne le théâtre classique. La répugnance à se donner en spectacle ne diffère guère du refus de parler' ('Les Ecarts de Trézène', in *Relectures raciniennes: Nouvelles Approches du discours tragique*, ed. R. L. Barnett (Paris — Seattle — Tübingen, 1986), 81–97, (p.93).

3 Henri Gouhier defines the essence of theatre as 'action' and 'le lieu où l'on voit' (*L'Existence et le théâtre* (Paris 1952), p.13). André Veinstein comments on Gouhier's perspective of theatre that that theatre is 'la présence de l'acteur' and that 'C'est en cette présence réelle...que Gouhier fait résider, pour une partie essentielle, la spécificité du théâtre' (*La Mise en scène théâtrale et sa condition esthétique* (Paris, 1955), p.208). For Starobinski the Racinian stage is where 'le vide est fait, sans objet interposé, et ce vide semble n'exister que pour être traversé de regards' ('Racine et la poétique du regard', in *L'Œil vivant* (Paris,

1970), p.75). For me a necessary component of presence is a stage where characters 'talk out' an issue: they cannot simply 'see' it out.

4 This leads her later to ask Zatime: 'Vois-tu dans ses discours qu'ils s'entendent tous deux?' (l. 1252) Sight and sound are allied in Antiochus's fear that: 'Je la verrai gémir' (l. 812). Néron warns Junie: 'J'entendrai des regards que vous croirez muets' (l. 682).

5 R. Emory makes the point that: 'Characters rarely ask if one has spoken to another, but rather has one *seen* him or her' ('*Bérénice* and the Language of Sight', *Romance Notes* 19 (1978–79), 217–22 (p.219)). I would argue that in any case speaking is a *necessary* complement of seeing.

6 J.A. Damart makes the perceptive point that: 'the one to whom she does not want to listen is only too ready to talk, whereas the one she desperately wants to hear avoids discussion as long as he can' ('The Power of the Spoken Word in *Bérénice*', *Romanic Review*, 67 (1976), 159–71 (p.160)). Damart also comments on the dichotomy in Racine's use of the eyes and mouth in *Bérénice*.

7 *Sur Racine* (Paris, 1963), pp.96–97.

8 Scherer describes Phèdre's confession, from my point of view felicitously, as an 'impudique mise au jour' *(Racine*, p.73).

9 For a view which stresses the 'immateriality' of Racine's tragedies see Ralph Albanese Jr., 'Dramaturgie classique et codes idéologiques: le cas Racine', in Barnett, op. cit. (pp.15–29). Anne Ubersfeld, on the other hand, argues: 'le visage et, tout particulièrement la bouche, est si l'on peut dire le lieu de rencontre entre la parole et le corps' *(L'Ecole du spectateur: Lire le théâtre 2* (Paris, 1981), p.223). Spitzer says of sight what could be said of 'bouche': 'Racine's *voir* is is neither entirely concrete nor entirely mental, and in this sense, it is perfectly characteristic of an art that is neither coarsely material nor entirely devoid of physicality' ('Racine's Classical *Piano*' in *Essays on Seventeenth-Century French Literature*, translated and edited by D. Bellos (Cambridge, 1983), 1–113 (p.38).

10 'Language and Power: Eyes and Words in Britannicus', *Yale French Studies* (45 (1970), 102–12 (p.102)

11 An excellent discussion of hyperbole is contained in Peter France, 'L'Hyperbole chez Racine', in *Racine: théâtre et poésie: Actes du Troisième Colloque Vinaver* (Manchester 1987), ed. Christine M. Hill (Leeds,1991), 23–35.

12 For further consideration of this point, see Maskell, pp.149–53.

13 J. Scherer comments: 'les personnages ne peuvent que parler, mais ils ne peuvent aucunement se fier à la parole, qui les englue et les engage dans des impasses ou des contradictions' *(Racine,* p.75).

14 These are ll.185–86, 237–38, 525–26 and 785–86. The others I have noted are: *Andromaque,* 1129–30, *Britannicus,* 747–48 and *Bérénice,* 883–84.

15 Richard Parish talks of 'signifying silence in spite of itself', '"Un Calme si funeste": Some Types of Silence in Racine', *French Studies,* 34 (1980), 385–400 (p.396).

16 Y. Pihan comments that: 'Aisément interprété ou non, le silence (chez Racine) ne laisse jamais indifférent, car toujours on le devine chargé de sens' ('Essai sur la poétique du silence chez Racine', *Cahiers raciniens,* 16 (1964), 41–55 (p.49))

17 This discussion was first elaborated in my article 'The Theatricality of Discourse in Racinian Tragedy' *MLR,* 84 (1989), 37–50. See also Maskell, pp.144–54.

18 Spitzer relates seeing to listening in *Andromaque* in the following comment: 'The repetition of *voir* indicates the importance placed by the speaker on his hearer's testimony' (p.37).

19 Damart is surely wrong in interpreting 'entendre' and 'écouter' as '*passive* equivalents' of 'parler' (his underlining) (p.159). Equally, Nina Ekstein cannot be right when she comments: 'The addressee's influence on the spectator is not surprising because both occupy similar passive positions vis-à-vis the communicative acts being performed, narrative or otherwise' *(Dramatic Narrative: Racine's 'Récits'* (New York, 1986) p.10.

20 Of Phèdre's confession, Barthes writes: 'C'est ici l'être même de la parole qui est porté sur le théâtre: la plus profonde des tragédies raciniennes est aussi la plus formelle; car l'enjeu tragique est ici beaucoup moins le sens de la parole que son apparition, beaucoup moins l'amour de Phèdre que son aveu' (p.67). This is the perspective in which I would place the whole of Racine's theatre.

21 See Maskell, pp.38–39 for comments on sound effects. Odette de Mourgues plays down the notion of sound in the plays: 'We do not find any of those distinctive utterances which some other dramatists use to convey emotion: no shrieks, no shouting, not a groan of pain' (*Racine or the Triumph of Relevance* (Cambridge, 1967), p.139).

22 See Chapter 3 of Maskell for a thorough review of gesture in Racine.

23 See Bernard Dort's article 'Huis-clos racinien', in *Cahiers de la Compagnie Madeleine Renaud — Jean-Louis Barrault* (1985), 7–16.

24 Retrospective stage directions are dealt with by Maskell, pp.65–6.

25 Eugène Vinaver noted this phenomenon: 'Les personnages s'écoutent au moins autant qu'ils écoutent les autres...la vengeance d'Hermione, sa décision irrévocable de faire périr Pyrrhus, ne vient pas d'un simple jeu d'arguments, mais des paroles mêmes qu'elle prononce: c'est au contact de ces paroles que le cœur d'Hermione retrouve toute sa violence et achève de l'égarer, comme si l'écho de sa voix se faisait complice de sa perte' *(Entretiens sur Racine* (Paris, 1984), p.65).

26 For Vinaver this line contains within itself all one can say on the real function of language in the tragedies: 'son rôle actif, sa puissance secrète qui fait qu'il suffit au personnages de la (=la parole) trouver pour se condamner' (*Entretiens,* p.71).

27 As J.C. Lapp comments on character in Racine: 'his safety depends upon his ability to interpret correctly the words, gestures, and expressions of his fellows at the same time as he masks his own feelings and intentions' *(Aspects of Racinian Tragedy* (Toronto, 1955), p.134).

28 For Scherer's definition of soliloquy, and its frequency in classical and Racinian tragedy, see *La Dramaturgie classique en France* (Paris, 1950), pp.245–65.

29 Benveniste defines the monologue as follows: Le monologue est un dialogue intériorisé, formulé en "langage intérieur", en un moi locuteur et un moi écouteur. Parfois le moi locuteur est seul à parler; le moi écouteur reste néanmoins présent; sa présence est nécessaire et suffisante pour rendre signifiante l'énonciation du moi locuteur. Parfois aussi le moi écouteur intervient par une objection, une question, un doute, une insulte' (quoted by Patrice Pavis in *Voix et images de la scène: Essais de sémiologie théâtrale* (Lille, 1982), p.50).

Notes to Chapter 3

1 See Spencer, p.259 for a perceptive view of the role of Antiochus as messenger in *Bérénice.* Indeed, the whole section on Antiochus is most useful for an understanding of the function of this character in the play.

2 Other considerations of space in *Bérénice* can be found in James J. Supple, *Racine: Phèdre* (London, 1986), pp.13sq.

3 Vinaver notes the difference between the two voices of Pyrrhus: 'Ecoutons cette nouvelle voix de Pyrrhus qui ressemble si peu à celle que Racine lui avait d'abord prêtée' *(Entretiens,* p.26).

4 An analysis of recognition in Racine is to be found in Terence Cave, *Recognitions: A Study in Poetics* (Oxford, 1988), pp.103–09.

5 Ubersfeld's comment on this aspect of character in general resembles my own view but more from the strict point of view of the semiotics of theatrical discourse: 'Ce qu'il est convenu d'appeler le conflit intérieur

du personnage est au théâtre collision de discours: à chaque pas nous nous heurtons à ce fait fondateur que, même dans le monologue, le discours du personnage n'est pas une coulée continue, mais la juxtaposition de couches textuelles différentes, qui entrent en rapport, en général conflictuel' *(Lire*, p.255).

6 Vinaver makes the following telling observation: 'non seulement sans Aricie (Hippolyte) n'aurait jamais formé ses vœux d'amour, mais jamais autrement qu'à l'aide d'un dialogue avec elle il n'aurait su les prononcer. C'est là, si l'on veut, la justification même de la forme dialoguée qui se charge ici de faire avancer l'action' *(Entretiens*, p.97).

7 Hubert extends this notion of displacement in the case of Hippolyte and his father: 'En tout cas, (Hippolyte) voudrait "ravir à la mémoire / Cette indigne moitié d'une si belle histoire" (93–94), ce qui reviendrait à réécrire la vie de son père *ad usum Delphini* [...] Dans un sens, il se rend coupable de détournement de mythe par substitution et déplacement' (Barnett, p.85).

8 For an interpretation of 'lire' in Racinian tragedy, see my article 'Racinian Letters', *Forum for Modern Language Studies*, 27 (1991), 35–42.

9 Poulet has the following to say about a character inhabited by two contradictory selves: 'Derrière la question *Qui suis-je*? il y a donc une question plus grave encore, et qui a rapport à l'effrayante impossibilité d'établir un rapport entre deux versions de soi-même que l'esprit confronte dans l'ordre des temps. La tragédie racinienne est faite, au moins partiellement, de cette incompréhensible incompatibilité qui se manifeste dans la conscience, lorsque les circonstances forcent soudainement un être à comparer deux moments inconciliables de sa propre durée' *(Mesure de l'instant* (Paris, 1968), p.58). In Chapter 4 I shall relate being as speech to the notion of time and duration in the tragedies.

Notes to Chapter 4

1 Hubert comments that the term 'éternel': 'n'a sans doute rien à voir avec la notion d'une durée infinie, mais exprime plutôt l'atemporalité, dans un sens théologique et mystique; seule la promesse de Dieu peut échapper à l'esclavage du temps. Nous n'avons vraiment que deux adversaires en présence: l'*atemporalité* divine et la *temporalité* humaine (Barnett, pp.76–77).

2 Poulet notes the repetitive structure of *Andromaque*: 'Aucune œuvre n'a exprimé plus complètement la puissance répétitive de la durée' (*Etudes sur le temps humain* (Paris, 1952), p.152).

3 See Van Delft, p.171.

4 Ubersfeld too conceives of an 'hors temps' but in a very different context to my own use of a similar term in English. Indeed, the whole chapter on time in *Lire le théâtre* should be read in conjunction with my analysis of speech in time.

5 See Phillips, *Racine: Mithridate* (London, 1990), Chapters 3 and 5 for a fuller discussion of this issue.

Notes to Conclusion

1 See *Word as Action: Racine, Rhetoric and Theatrical Language* (Oxford, 1992).

2 See in particular Maurice Delcroix, 'La Tragédie de Racine est-elle psychologique?', in *Racine: Mythes et réalités* (Actes du *Colloque Racine* tenu à l'Université de Western Ontario, London, Canada, en mars 1974), (London, 1976), 104–119.

3 *Héros et orateurs: Rhétorique et dramaturgie cornéliennes* (Geneva, 1990), p.508.

Selective Bibliography

Alabanese Jr, R. 'Dramaturgie classique et codes idéologiques: le cas Racine', Barnett, 15–29.

Barnett, R. L. (ed.) *Relectures raciniennes: Nouvelles Approches du discours tragique* (Paris — Seattle — Tübingen, 1986).

Barthes, R. *Sur Racine* (Paris, 1963).

Cave, T. *Recognitions: A Study in Poetics* (Oxford, 1988).

Czarnecki, M. 'Jouer / parler Racine (*Andromaque*)', *Comédie française*, 115 (1983), 18–20.

Damart, J. A. 'The Power of the Spoken Word in *Bérénice*', *Romanic Review*, 67 (1976), 159–71,

Delcroix, M. 'La Tragédie de Racine est-elle psychologique?', in *Racine: Mythes et réalités* (Actes du *Colloque Racine* tenu à l'Université de Western Ontario, London, Canada, en mars 1974), (London, 1976), 104–119.

Dort, B. 'Huis-clos racinien', *Cahiers de la Compagnie Madeleine Renaud — Jean-Louis Barrault* (1985), 7–16.

Ekstein, Nina C. *Dramatic Narrative: Racine's 'Récits'* (New York, 1986).

Emory, R. '*Bérénice* and the Language of Sight', *Romance Notes*, 19 (1978–79), 217–22.

France, P. *Racine's Rhetoric* (Oxford, 1965).

'L'Hyperbole chez Racine', *Racine: théâtre et poésie. Actes du Troisième Colloque Vinaver (Manchester 1987)*, ed. Christine M. Hill (Leeds,1991), 23–35.

Freeman, B. C. and Batson, A. *Concordance du théâtre et des poésies de Jean Racine* (Ithaca, 1968).

Fumaroli, M. *Héros et Orateurs: Rhétorique et dramaturgie cornéliennes* (Paris, 1990)

Gouhier, H. *L'Existence et le théâtre* (Paris, 1952).

Heyndels, I. *Le Conflit racinien: Esquisse d'un système tragique* (Brussels, 1985).

Howarth, W. D. 'L'Alexandrin classique comme instrument du dialogue théâtral', *Langage dramatique: dramaturgie. Mélanges offerts à Jacques Scherer* (Paris, 1986), 341–54.

Hubert, Judd D. *Essai d'exégèse racinienne: Bérénice, Bajazet, Athalie* (Paris, 1985).

'Les Ecarts de Trézène', in Barnett, pp. 81–97.

Kennedy, A. *Dramatic Dialogue* (Cambridge, 1983).

Lapp. J. C. *Aspects of Racinian Tragedy* (Toronto, 1955).

Larthomas, P. *Le Langage dramatique: Sa Nature, ses procédés* (Paris, 1972).

Macarthur, Elizabeth J. 'Trading Genres: Epistolarity and Theatricality in *Britannicus* and *Les Liaisons dangereuses*', *Yale French Studies,* 76 (1989), 243–64.

Maskell, D. *Racine: a Theatrical Reading* (Oxford, 1991).

Maulnier Th. *Racine* (Paris, 1947).

Mourgues, O. de, *Racine or the Triumph of Relevance* (Cambridge, 1967).

Parish, R. *Racine: the Limits of Tragedy* (Paris — Seattle — Tübingen, 1993).

'"Un Calme si funeste": Some Types of Silence in Racine', *French Studies,* 34 (1980), 385–400.

Pavis, P. *Voix et images de la scène: Essais de sémiologie théâtrale* (Lille, 1982).

Phillips, H. *Racine: Mithridate* (London, 1990).

'The Theatricality of Discourse in Racinian Tragedy', *MLR,* 84 (1989), 37–50.

'Racinian Letters', *Forum for Modern Language Studies*, 27 (1991), 35–42.

'Racinian Tragedy: Text as Theatre', *Racine: Appraisal and Reappraisal* (Bristol, 1991), 25–37.

'Language, Voice and Substitution in Racine', *Voices in the Air: French Dramatists and the Resources of Language. Essays in Honour of Charles Chadwick,* ed. John Dunkley and Bill Kirton (Glasgow, 1992), 1–13.

Pihan, Y. 'Essai sur la poétique du silence chez Racine', *Cahiers raciniens*, 16 (1964), 41–55.

Poulet, G. *Etudes sur le temps humain* (Paris, 1952).

La Mesure de l'instant (Paris, 1968).

Racine, J. *Théâtre complet*, ed. J. Morel and A. Viala (Paris, 1980).

Ratermanis, J. B. *Essai sur les formes verbales dans les tragédies de Racine* (Paris, 1972).

Scherer, J. *La Dramaturgie classique en France* (Paris, 1950).

Racine et / ou la cérémonie (Paris, 1982).

Spencer, C. *La Tragédie du Prince. Etude du personnage médiateur dans le théâtre tragique de Racine* (Paris — Seattle — Tübingen, 1987).

Spitzer, L. 'Racine's Classical *Piano*' in *Essays on Seventeenth-Century French Literature*, translated and edited by D. Bellos (Cambridge, 1983), 1–113.

Starobinski, J. 'Racine et la poétique du regard', in *L'Œil vivant* (Paris, 1970).

Ubersfeld, A. *Lire le théâtre* (Paris, 1977).

L'Ecole du spectateur: Lire le théâtre 2 (Paris, 1981)

Van Delft, L. 'Language and Power: Eyes and Words in *Britannicus*', *Yale French Studies*, 45 (1970), 102–12.

Veinstein, A. *La Mise en scène théâtrale et sa condition esthétique* (Paris, 1955).

Vinaver, E. *Racine et la Poésie tragique* (Paris, 1963).

Entretiens sur Racine (Paris, 1984).